Samuel Rutherford

Lover of Christ

Richard M. Hannula

 BOOKS

EP BOOKS
Faverdale North
Darlington
DL3 0PH, England

www.epbooks.org
sales@epbooks.org

EP BOOKS are distributed in the USA by:
JPL Fulfillment
3741 Linden Avenue Southeast,
Grand Rapids, MI 49548.

E-mail: sales@jplfulfillment.com
Tel: 877.683.6935

First published 2014

British Library Cataloguing in Publication Data available
ISBN: 978-1-78397-018-6

To my dear friends in Scotland

*— Angus, Mae, Heather, Iain, Angus John, Calum,
Findlay, Gillian, Kevin, Esther Mae and Naomi —*

*with gratitude for your warm fellowship
and gracious hospitality.*

Contents

Introduction

In 1636, King Charles I and Archbishop Laud escalated their plans to foist a foreign, English episcopacy and high-church ceremonies on the Church of Scotland. A kingdom-wide crackdown on nonconformists — those who viewed the king's demands as unbiblical and refused to accept them — swept up a number of the most outspoken opponents. Foremost among them was Samuel Rutherford. In Edinburgh in August 1636, Rutherford received the verdict of the Court of High Commission. The outcome of his three-day trial for nonconformity was never in doubt. The bishops, doing the bidding of King Charles I, wished to be rid of the staunch supporter of the Crown Rights of King Jesus. The court declared him guilty, expelled him from his pastorate, banned him from preaching and exiled him to Aberdeen until the king's pleasure should deem otherwise.

As the thirty-six-year-old Rutherford left the courtroom, he wondered if his usefulness to Christ and his Church had come to an end. He confessed to a friend that he felt like 'an outcast and a withered tree'. Little could he have known that his exile would end in less than two years when Scotland rose up to resist the king's domination of the church. He could hardly have imagined that he would serve a key role in reasserting biblical doctrine, worship and government to the Scottish church. He would also play an important part in the Westminster Assembly, defining Christian doctrine for much of the English-speaking world for centuries to come, and nearly two dozen influential books would flow from his pen, winning the admiration of the Reformed churches of Britain and the Continent. He would even have the most prestigious universities in the Netherlands and Scotland clamour to have him fill their chairs of divinity, and as a professor of theology, he would mould the minds of a generation of Scottish pastors and theologians.

Alexander Whyte wrote: 'No man of his age in broad Scotland stood higher as a scholar, a theologian, a controversialist, a preacher and a very saint than Samuel Rutherford.'

Nor could Rutherford have envisioned in his wildest dreams that a collection of letters that he sent to friends from his exile in Aberdeen would rank among the most beloved Christian classics, a timeless source of spiritual inspiration to millions of readers.

His incredibly productive and fruitful life was punctuated with tragedy, suffering and loss. His first wife died in her early twenties, and eight of his nine children perished in childhood. Three times the authorities forced him to abandon his ministerial labours. Twice he was called to the bar to stand trial for his faith. A fatal illness kept Rutherford from facing public execution for Christ on the gallows of Edinburgh.

Yet through it all, his deep love for his Saviour shone like a beacon. 'You shall see that one look of Christ's sweet and lovely eye,' he wrote to a friend from exile, 'one kiss of His fairest face is worth 10,000 worlds of such a rotten stuff as the foolish sons of men set their hearts upon.'

One of his biographers, surveying the great personalities of church history, asked: 'Who is so transported and lost to himself in the beauty and sweetness of Christ as Samuel Rutherford?'

'Welcome,' Rutherford said, 'welcome Jesus, in what way so ever thou come, if we can get a sight of Thee.'

More than three and a half centuries after his death, Rutherford's life and letters continue to show Christ for all who have eyes to see him.

Timeline

1600	Approximate date of Rutherford's birth
1603	Union of the Crowns — James VI of Scotland becomes James I of England
1610	King James established bishops in the Church of Scotland by royal authority
1617	Rutherford began his studies at University of Edinburgh
1618	Five Articles of Perth enacted
1623	Rutherford appointed Professor of Humanities at University of Edinburgh
1625	James I died — succeeded by his son Charles I; Rutherford resigned from the University under accusations of an ethics violation

1627	Rutherford ordained and installed as the minister of Anwoth Parish
1630	Rutherford's wife and child died
1636	Rutherford's book against Arminianism published; Rutherford deposed from his pulpit and exiled to Aberdeen
1637	Scots refused to accept Laud's Liturgy
1638	National Covenant signed; Rutherford left Aberdeen; Presbyterianism re-established in Scotland
1638	Church of Scotland's General Assembly assigned Rutherford to St Andrews University
1639–40	The Bishops' Wars
1642–48	First and Second Civil Wars
1643	Solemn League and Covenant signed
1643–49	Westminster Assembly wrote the confession of faith and the catechisms
1644	*Lex, Rex* published
1649	English Parliament executed King Charles I
1651	Scots crowned Charles II at Scone; Cromwell

defeated Scottish forces and imposed a military governor over Scotland; Protester and Resolutioner Controversy divides the Church of Scotland

1660   Restoration of the Stuart Monarchy; *Lex, Rex* condemned; Rutherford deposed from St Andrews University

1661   Rutherford charged with treason, but he died in St Andrews before he could stand trial; Rule of Bishops re-established by law in the Church of Scotland; the Reverend James Guthrie, first Covenanter, executed

1664   *Rutherford's Letters* published for the first time

1

University

"'Whoever drinks of the water that I will give him will never be thirsty again. The water that I will give him will become in him a spring of water welling up to eternal life'"
(John 4:14).

Samuel Rutherford was born around 1600 in Nisbet, a small village in the border country of south-eastern Scotland located a few miles from Jedburgh. The rich farmland, green hills and rushing streams shaped Rutherford's love of nature. His father, a farmer of some means, saw to the education of his sons.

The earliest recorded event of Rutherford's life sounds more like legend than fact. It seems that the four-year-old Samuel was playing with some friends near the village well. While he absentmindedly scrambled around the edge of the deep well, he fell in. His friends ran for help. When they returned, they found Samuel sitting on a knoll, soaking wet but uninjured. When they asked him how he escaped, he told them, 'A bonnie white man came and drew me out of the well!'

Andrew Bonar, a nineteenth-century Scottish pastor, said of this incident, 'Whether or not he really fancied that an angel had delivered him, we cannot tell; but it is plain that his boyish thoughts were already wandering in the region of the sky.' Certainly, generations of Scots who heard this story assumed that an angel rescued the boy who was destined by God's plan to play a great role in the Scottish church.

Young Samuel and his brothers went to school in the old monastery of Jedburgh. Jedburgh Abbey, founded by King David I of Scotland in the twelfth century, had been one of the largest monasteries in the land and was the finest example of Romanesque architecture in Scotland. Not long after the Scottish Reformation of 1560, the monks left the abbey, and the sanctuary became the worship site for the town's Reformed church. Part of the mammoth building housed a grammar school. The sight of the great round arches, massive stone pillars and high walls must have been awe-inspiring to the students, who would have seen few man-made structures larger than a barn.

The decades before Rutherford's birth and the years of his childhood brought sweeping changes to the Scottish church. Under the leadership of John Knox in the 1560s and 70s, the Scots threw off the shackles of medieval Roman Catholicism and established a national church based on the teachings of the Bible. Knox, who had lived in exile in Geneva, embraced the theology of the reformer John Calvin, himself an exile from France. Knox called Calvin's Geneva 'the most perfect school of Christ that was ever on earth since the days of the apostles.'

Unlike in England where King Henry VIII, as head of the church, kept a tight rein on how much change he would permit the reformers to implement, the early decades of the Scottish Reformation developed without the interference of the monarch shaping its doctrine and practice. Knox and the reformers who followed after him concentrated their efforts on providing pastors for the Scottish churches who would faithfully preach the Word of God and provide spiritual nurture to their flocks. They organized Christian schools in hundreds of parishes, which enlightened and revolutionized Scotland, pulling it out of a centuries-old fog of superstition and ignorance. The Scottish reformers rejected the hierarchal system of the Roman Catholic Church and established a Presbyterian system of church government where all ministers were of equal rank. Ministers and elders, chosen by each congregation, ruled the local body and served in the higher courts of the church, called presbyteries and general assemblies.

Knox and his successor Andrew Melville made it clear that the monarch of Scotland had no rule in the church. 'There are two kings and two kingdoms in Scotland,' Melville once told King James. 'There is King James, the head of the commonwealth; and there is Christ Jesus, the King of the Kirk, whose subject James VI is, and of whose kingdom he is not a king, nor a lord, nor a head, but a member.'

But as King James VI entered his adulthood — he was crowned king at the age of one and a regent reigned in his name until he reached the age of majority — he began to claim his authority in the church. James did not trust the independence of the Presbyterian Kirk nor did he like an influential institution in his realm to be outside his control. Guided by his faith in the divine right of kings — the belief that monarchs had absolute authority from God to rule over church and state — James resented the bold Presbyterian ministers who preached about the rights of King Jesus in his Kirk. The king said that Presbyterianism agreed with monarchy as much as God agreed with the devil. A few years later, he uttered his famous phrase, 'No bishop, no king.'

According to James: 'To dispute what God may do is blasphemy, so it is to dispute what a king may do in the height of his power.' Over time, he took incremental steps to place the Church of Scotland under his control.

In 1584, James pushed through a compliant Scottish Parliament the so-called 'Black Acts' which declared the king's authority in the church. The Acts forbade the convening of church councils or general assemblies to decide any matters without the king's permission. They made it a crime to speak privately against the Crown or to preach from the pulpit anything contrary to the king's policies. Finally, the Acts empowered the Archbishop of St Andrews to oversee the nation's churches and determine the fitness of candidates for the ministry.

The General Assembly of the Church of Scotland, refusing to stand by idly, pushed back and demanded a true Presbyterian form of government where power rested with ministers and elders, not bishops set above the parish ministers. This began years of wrestling between the General Assembly and the king and his bishops for control of the church. In 1592, the jurisdiction of bishops was abolished again and general assemblies won the right to meet every year at a time and place appointed by the king. But James did not give up, asserting at opportune times his influence in church affairs.

In 1603, when Samuel Rutherford was just a toddler, Queen Elizabeth of England died. She had never married and so had no direct descendants to inherit her crown. England turned to her cousin, King James of Scotland, as the closest heir to the throne. James VI of Scotland then moved to London and ruled the kingdoms jointly as King James I of England and James VI of Scotland.

When James set up his court at Westminster, he found the fawning, compliant English prelates much to his liking. He recognized that the English ecclesiastical system with the monarch as the supreme governor of the church strengthened the power of the Crown. His Scottish Presbyterian subjects had regularly resisted his interference in the church and were not afraid to put James in his place. Once when in the midst of an argument with King James, Andrew Melville grabbed James's sleeve and called him 'God's silly vassal'. But few English ministers dared to challenge him so boldly.

Soon James determined to bring about a complete civil and ecclesiastical union of his kingdoms. Although they shared a common king, Scotland was an independent country from England, and the Scottish Reformation had gone much further in reforming the church according to the Bible than had the Church of England. With the power of the throne of England behind him, James forced the rule of Crown-appointed bishops on Scotland and tried to abolish general assemblies altogether. The Scots resisted the imposition of a foreign church government upon them which they viewed as contrary to the Scriptures. When Andrew Melville spoke out against the foisting of the English church system on Scotland, James exiled him, and threw some other Presbyterian leaders in prison. But James's Scottish bishops advised him that the church would revolt if he exercised too heavy a hand. They urged him to take a patient approach to change the Church of Scotland.

Meanwhile, after young Samuel Rutherford had demonstrated his skill in Latin, the language used in college lectures and readings, he was admitted to the University of Edinburgh in 1617. The gifted seventeen-year-old with blond curls and bright eyes excelled in the rigorous course of study which required eight to ten hours in the classroom each day. He mastered the Greek and Latin classics, logic, philosophy, theology and science.

During his university days, it appears that Rutherford suddenly came to a clear and saving faith in Christ. 'O, but Christ hath a saving eye!' he said. 'When He first looked on me I was saved; it cost Him but a look to make hell quit to me!'

He felt a bond of love with the Saviour from the start. 'Since He looked upon me,' Rutherford explained, 'my heart is not my own; He hath run away to heaven with it.'

In his adulthood, he lamented wasting much of his youth before following Christ's narrow way. 'Like a fool as I was,' he wrote, 'I suffered my sun to be high in the heaven and near afternoon before ever I took the gate by the end.'

After four years, Rutherford earned a Masters of Arts degree and two years later in 1623, despite strong competition from older and more experienced men, the University of Edinburgh appointed him Professor of Humanities. His primary duties included teaching Latin and Greek, and lecturing on Roman literature.

Meanwhile, King James proceeded to impose his long-ripening plan on the Church of Scotland. In 1618, James demanded that the Scottish Kirk adopt several elements of Anglican worship. Under threats from the king, an assembly of noblemen and churchmen in Perth obligingly enacted changes to the practices of the church known as the Five Articles. However, most of the ministers voted against them. The Articles approved practices that included kneeling to receive the bread and wine at the Lord's Supper, the private use of the sacraments, confirmation of young people at the hands of a bishop and the observance of holy days appointed by the church hierarchy.

Many Scots and their ministers refused to accept the Five Articles of Perth, believing the articles were not taught in Scripture. Some were dragged before the Court of High Commission and fined, and a few pastors were removed from their pulpits. But most Scottish bishops did not go out of their way to enforce the Articles, hoping that over time the people and clergy would accept the changes. James knew enough of the character of the Scottish people not to press them too hard.

While in Edinburgh, Rutherford associated closely with the defenders of Presbyterianism. Beyond the college walls, he met with merchants, nobles and others who worked to mobilize support to rid the Church of Scotland of the rule of bishops and return her to Presbyterian government and the doctrines of the Reformation. They gathered privately to worship, pray and strategize.

After Rutherford began his university teaching, he married Eupham Hamilton. But soon a scandal arose in connection with his marriage. According to the Edinburgh city records from 3 February 1626, the principal of the university reported that Samuel Rutherford had 'fallen in fornication with Eupham Hamilton and he has committed a great scandal in the college'.

Was it true that Eupham was pregnant before their wedding? Or was it, as some biographers contend, that Rutherford had simply married without the requisite permission of the university and the church hierarchy in Edinburgh? Or was it a ruse of the Episcopal party to raise doubts about Rutherford to remove a staunch Presbyterian from a position of influence? Whatever the facts were, Rutherford resigned his professorship under a cloud.

Whether this episode wracked his conscience or not, it is clear that for the rest of his life Rutherford remembered with regret and repentance the sins of his younger years. 'The old ashes of the sins of my youth are a new fire of sorrow to me,' he said.

Later he counselled a parent, 'The hot fiery lusts and passions of youth are much to be feared.'

In 1625, King James died, and his son Charles ascended to the throne. King Charles I embraced his father's view of absolute monarchy. Charles grew up in England and did not understand the character of the Scottish people or their Kirk. A high-church Anglican, Charles had married a French Roman Catholic princess, and despised English Puritans and Scottish Presbyterians. Although it took him a few years to implement his plans, he sought to dominate the Church of Scotland more than his father had dared to do.

In April 1626, shortly after Rutherford resigned his post at the University of Edinburgh, his wife gave birth to their first child, a daughter named Marie. A year later, Rutherford left the capital and accepted a call to become the minister of a small country church.

2

Anwoth

'His banner over me was love'
(Song of Solomon 2:4).

During Rutherford's final years teaching at the University of Edinburgh, he also studied theology and prepared for the ministry. By 1627, he had been licensed by the Church of Scotland as a preacher of the gospel, and he accepted a call to Anwoth in Galloway. In early spring, Samuel Rutherford, Eupham and Marie settled into the manse.

The patron of Anwoth parish was Sir John Gordon, a strong supporter of Scottish Presbyterianism. As a result of the Scottish Reformation in the 1560s, noblemen had gained land formerly owned by the Catholic Church. The Gordons, one of the most prominent families in south-west Scotland, obtained possession of a large tract of church land once controlled by the Bishop of Galloway. Lord Gordon harboured great suspicions of the king's designs on the Scottish church, and he feared the growing power of the bishops.

Galloway had been a centre of Presbyterian strength for fifty years. John Welsh, John Knox's son-in-law and the long-serving preacher at Kirkcudbright, a town seven miles from Anwoth, promoted the Reformed faith in the region. Before Rutherford arrived, Anwoth shared with a neighbouring parish a minister named William Dalgleish. Dalgleish taught them the true gospel of Christ and inculcated in them an appreciation for Presbyterian government and Reformed worship. Many poor cottagers, as well as the ruling class, accepted his teaching. They only wished they could hear him more often, complaining that they suffered the 'miserable famine of the Word receiving only the poor help of one sermon every second Sabbath'.

When Gordon received permission from the Church of Scotland to make Anwoth a separate parish, he wanted to place a staunch Presbyterian in the pulpit. Gordon extracted a promise from Bishop Lamb of Galloway, a moderate Episcopalian, that he would not force the church of Anwoth to adopt episcopal ceremonies.

Initially, Lord Gordon asked a man named John Livingstone to lead the church. However, a variety of circumstances led Livingstone to decline the position. Livingstone went on to become a famous preacher and the instrument of a great revival of faith in Christ. Gordon's second choice was Samuel Rutherford. Years later, the humble Livingstone wrote about his turning down the call to Anwoth: 'The Lord provided a great deal better for them; for they got that worthy servant of Christ, Mr Samuel Rutherford, whose praise is in all the Reformed churches.'

When John Gordon presented to the congregation Samuel Rutherford as a candidate for the Anwoth pulpit, they wholeheartedly voted in favour of him. Rutherford believed that the approval of the flock was essential to any minister's call. 'The lawful calling of a pastor to the flock of Christ,' Rutherford said, 'requires the consent and approbation of the people and the presbytery.' This was a sharp contrast to the episcopal system in which pastors were chosen by bishops without input from the people.

Anwoth parish, tucked between the foothills of the Southern Uplands and the waters of the Solway Firth, spanned many square miles of green hills and narrow valleys. The church building was set in a basin edged by trees. The barn-shaped, stone sanctuary was not large — sixty feet by eighteen feet — and was capable of holding just over 200 people. One end wall of the church included a short tower which housed a small bell. A simple oak pulpit and communion table stood at the front.

The manse, known as Bush-o-Bield, was a large old stone building, formerly the manor house of a minor noble. It was surrounded by gigantic holly bushes with a stream flowing through the garden. Rutherford's small family occupied a fraction of the rooms. Ash, pine and other trees lined the path that linked the manse to the church.

Rutherford entered his labours at Anwoth with boundless energy. He rose at three o'clock every morning to spend several hours in prayer, meditation, Bible study and sermon preparation. As part of his daily routine, he walked the dirt

trail between the manse and the church to pray under a
thick canopy of branches. His parishioners often saw him
deep in prayer, treading the footpath with his eyes toward
heaven. They came to call this pathway 'Rutherford's Walk'.

'There, I wrestled with the angel and prevailed,' Rutherford
said of his retreat. 'Woods, trees, meadows, and hills are my
witness that I drew as a fair meeting between Christ and
Anwoth.'

The parish had no village centre. If Rutherford was going
to get to know his flock, he would have to tramp the hills
and hollows to visit them in their isolated cottages scattered
across the countryside. Every afternoon, he could be
found winding his way through the ferns and heather of a
mountainside or wading through streams to meet his people.
He talked with his parishioners about Christ as they herded
sheep on the dewy slopes or harvested their meagre crops
from the fields. Rutherford read the Scriptures aloud and
expounded them to women spinning wool by their hearths,
and catechized their children round the fire. 'Salvation,
salvation is our only necessary thing,' he told them.

A minister friend said that Rutherford was 'one of the most
faithful and diligent ministers that ever laboured among a
people'.

It was apparent that Rutherford loved Christ and that he
longed for his people to love him too. He directed all his
efforts to that end. 'I must tell you what lovely Jesus, fair
Jesus, King Jesus, has done to my soul,' he said.

He urged his congregation to receive Christ. 'Take Him,' Rutherford preached, 'take Him then with God's blessing. God gave you Him with goodwill, take Him with heart and goodwill.'

Each day, he visited the bedsides of the sick and comforted the grieving. Rutherford took his calling seriously and ministered to his people as one who must give an account to God. He told a friend that concerns for his flock brought forth in him 'tears, cares, fears and daily prayers'.

Through tireless visitation, Rutherford grew intimately acquainted with his people, learning their strengths and failings and the challenges of their daily lives. He discovered how best to minister to them in the pulpit and in private conversation. Soon a deep bond of love formed between the pastor and his congregation. He called them 'My dear flock' and 'Beloved'. The feeling was reciprocal. The congregation wrote to the General Assembly commending Rutherford stating: 'God has blessed his labours among us. We find a mutual union of our hearts between him and us.'

Of particular interest to Rutherford was the spiritual welfare of children. He wrote a catechism to use with the young ones of his parish. 'I desire your children to seek the Lord,' he told parents, 'to come take Christ, and all things with Him.'

He implored fathers and mothers to lead their children to the Saviour. 'Christ is an unknown Christ to young ones,' he said, 'and therefore they seek Him not because they know Him not.'

Although Rutherford soon became known for his preaching, he did not look or sound the part of a powerful preacher. He was short, slight and preached in a high pitched voice — some described it as 'shrill'. But he vividly set Christ before his congregation, helping them to see Jesus Christ preaching, healing, bearing his cross, reigning in heaven and interceding for them. 'I beseech you in the Lord,' he pleaded, 'to give your soul no rest till you have real assurance, and Christ's rights confirmed and sealed to your soul.'

Wearing a black Genevan gown, Rutherford began each sermon with a thorough examination of the passage, highlighting its primary scriptural truths. Notwithstanding Rutherford's brilliance as a scholar, he proclaimed the Word of God in simple ways that poorly educated country folk could understand. He told his congregation that he laboured 'to warn and stir up their minds'.

He implored his congregation not to be passive listeners. 'Hang upon the Word,' Rutherford preached, 'but with all to look beyond the Word and with the use of the Word, call for the inward grace of the Spirit.'

The heart of nearly all his sermons was the cross of Jesus Christ and the glories of the Saviour. 'What a flower, what a Rose of light and love Christ is,' he exclaimed from the pulpit. 'Christ cannot but be an infinite and eternal flowing sea to let out streams and floods of boundless grace. O what a happiness for a soul to lose its excellency in His transcendent glory! What a blessedness for the creature to cast in his little all in Christ's matchless all-sufficiency!'

He found inspiration in the images of the Song of Songs, seeing the Song as a metaphor that depicted the love of Christ for his Church and for each individual believer. Using highly emotional, even sensual terms, Rutherford described the relationship between Christ and believers as a spiritual marriage. In his letters and sermons, he referred to 'Christ's soft and sweet kisses'. He often talked about embracing the Lord with tears and sighs. 'At the Lord's first meeting with the sinner,' he preached, 'the Lord opens his heart by grace to let Him in, and there they sit together. There is a feast of love between them.'

'O for eternity's leisure to look on Him,' he told his congregation, 'to feast upon the sight of his face! O for the long summer day of endless ages to stand beside Him and enjoy Him!'

'Why do Christ's friends commend Him so much?' Rutherford asked in a sermon. 'Even that you and He may fall in love together.'

A minister friend reported that preaching about Christ's love or the glories of heaven made Rutherford's 'face to shine' and brought a 'peculiar sweetness' to his speech. He surmised that Rutherford did not get this from his university education 'nor could flesh and blood reveal it to him — he was a student above the clouds'.

One man said that when Rutherford preached about Christ, it looked like he would fly out of the pulpit for joy.

'May the Lord Jehovah persuade you to embrace the offer,' he told his congregation, 'and flee into lovely Christ Jesus, the glorious Prince of renown, and to Him be praise for ever and ever.'

Even though Rutherford described himself as 'over head and ears in love with that princely one, Christ Jesus my Lord', he knew he was just scratching the surface of his Redeemer. 'Christ, all the seasons of the year, is dropping sweetness,' he said. 'If I had vessels I might fill them, but my old, riven, and running-out dish can bring a little. Alas! I have spilled more of Christ's grace, love, faith, humility and godly sorrow than I have brought with me. How little of the sea can a child carry in his hand; as little am I able to take away of my great Sea, my boundless and running-over Christ Jesus!'

'Every day,' he wrote, 'we may see some new thing in Christ; His love has neither brim nor bottom.'

Rutherford reported dreaming of Christ at night and talking about him in his sleep. 'Sometimes,' he wrote to his minister friend David Dickson, 'when I have Christ in my arms I fall asleep in the sweetness of His presence and when I awake, I miss Him.'

Mere words failed him as he strove to express the wonders of God and salvation. So Rutherford used extravagant language and large numbers to try to convey the magnitude of Christ and the glories of heaven: 'Therefore come near, and take a view of that transparent beauty that is in Christ,' he said, 'which would busy the love of 10,000 millions of worlds.'

'Put the beauty of 10,000 thousand worlds of paradises, like the Garden of Eden, in one,' he wrote, 'and all trees, all flowers, all smells, all colours, all tastes, all joys, all loveliness, all sweetness, in one. And yet it would be less to that fair and dearest well-beloved Christ, than one drop of rain to the whole seas, rivers, lakes and fountains of 10,000 earths.'

'You shall see that one look of Christ's sweet and lovely eye,' Rutherford exclaimed, 'one kiss of His fairest face is worth 10,000 worlds of such rotten stuff as the foolish sons of men set their hearts upon.'

'Millions of hells of sinners cannot come near to exhaust infinite grace,' Rutherford taught.

He rejoiced in preaching and viewed it as his greatest way to glorify Christ. 'I had but one joy out of heaven next to Christ my Lord, and that was to preach Him,' Rutherford said.

When he preached about Christ, his hearers described it as 'heart-melting'. He called preaching 'the apple of the eye of my delights'.

Once a noblewoman was asked why she travelled away from her parish to hear Rutherford. 'I go to Anwoth so often,' she said, 'because although other ministers show me the majesty of God and the plague of my own heart, Mr Samuel does both of these things, but he also shows me as no other minister does the loveliness of Christ.'

In his sermons, letters and conversations, Rutherford proclaimed salvation as a free and unmerited gift of God's grace. He liked to quote 2 Timothy 1:9: '[God] hath saved us, and called us with a holy calling, not according to our works, but according to His own purpose and grace, which was given us in Christ Jesus before the world began.'

He taught that repentance unto life was completely a supernatural gift from God. 'There is no man who can come out to meet Christ,' Rutherford preached, 'till first He come to him. No man can love Christ till He love him first, because our love of Christ is nothing else but an effect of His love to us ... so we may learn forever to sing a song of free grace shown in our conversion.'

'I am Christ's sworn bankrupt,' Rutherford wrote, 'to whom He will entrust nothing; no, not one pin in the work of salvation.'

'Be glad you are His own;' he preached to his flock, 'He won you with the sweat of His brow. It is true, you deserve not Christ, but indeed He deserves you. Therefore be glad and humble, for Christ will not lack His own.'

Rutherford preached warmly of Christ and forgiveness, but he also strongly denounced sin. 'How many are in the world,' he asked, 'who live and die in adultery and harlotry, living a profane and godless life, not making conscience of swearing, drinking, breaking the Lord's Day and so lose the right way to heaven?'

The power and status of Lord Gordon did not keep Rutherford from telling him the truth about his needy condition. 'Stoop, stoop!' Rutherford told him. 'It is a low entry to go in at heaven's gate.'

Knowing from the Scriptures that Christians must strive and struggle in their faith, he implored his people to trust in Christ and live for God. 'Take pains, above all things, for salvation,' he wrote, 'for without running, fighting, sweating, wrestling, heaven is not taken.'

Christ called all his followers, Rutherford said, 'to holy walking and acts of believing. You will not be carried to heaven lying at ease upon a feather bed.'

'Put off a sin, or a piece of it, every day,' he counselled his flock.

'Should you not then give your best things to Christ?' Rutherford asked in a sermon. 'For He gave the best things He had for you — even His precious blood; for the life is in the blood. He seeks no more but the blood and life of your heart-idols and sins; for, says He, "I slew myself for you, and if you love Me give blood for blood."'

Being all too aware from his own experience that young people were particularly vulnerable to temptation, Rutherford used vivid imagery to put them on their guard. 'There is not such a glassy, icy, slippery piece of way between you and heaven as youth,' he said.

'Beware of a green young devil,' he warned them. 'For in youth the devil finds dry sticks and dry coals and a hot hearth-stone, and how soon with his flint strikes fire, and with his bellows blow it up, and fire the house! Sanctified thoughts, thoughts made conscience of, and called in, and kept in awe are green fuel that burns not and are a water for Satan's coal.'

He urged his congregation to use the means of grace —
prayer, Bible study, corporate worship, fellowship — to grow
in Christ. 'Try and search His Word,' he advised. 'In the midst
of worldly employments,' Rutherford said, 'there should be
some thoughts of sin, death, judgement, and eternity, with a
word or two at least of ejaculatory prayer to God.'

'I pray you, beloved,' Rutherford preached, 'when you are
toiling at your farms, trafficking, or sporting, be asking God,
"Lord, how shall it go with me at the Last Judgment?"'

'I have now made a new question,' Rutherford wrote in a letter.
'Whether Christ is more to be loved for giving sanctification
or for free justification? And I hold that He is more and most
to be loved for sanctification. It is, in some respects, greater
love in Him to sanctify than to justify; for He makes us most
like Himself, in His own essential portraiture and image in
sanctifying us.'

All the good works that believers do, he reminded his flock,
are ultimately Christ's doing. 'In gospel obedience,' he said,
'we offer more of the Lord's own and less of our own.'

In a sermon, he advised his flock, 'Then learn under temptations to keep Christ on your side and not to take on the work
alone.'

In the pursuit of obedience, Rutherford warned, believers
should not lose their first love. 'Holiness is not Christ, nor
the blossoms and flowers of the tree of life, nor the tree
itself.'

Nor should they be discouraged with their slow progress in holiness because Christ is still at work in them. 'I am a wretched captive of sin,' Rutherford confessed, 'yet my Lord can hew heaven out of worse timber than I am, if worse there be.'

There should be no sense of self-accomplishment in the Christian life, Rutherford emphasized. 'There cannot be a more humble soul than a believer;' he told a fellow minister, 'it is no pride for a drowning man to catch hold of a rock.'

Although the people liked Rutherford from the start, few, at first, came to faith in Christ through his witness. After two years in Anwoth, he wrote: 'I see exceedingly small fruit of my ministry. I would be glad of one soul to be my crown of joy in the day of Christ.'

He lamented the iron grip that the world had on so many of his people. 'It is not our part to make a treasure here,' he said. 'Anything under the covering of heaven which we can build upon is but ill ground and a sandy foundation.'

Rutherford told them that the pleasures of this life would disappear as quickly 'as a snowball melted away'.

'Many do with Jesus Christ as onlookers do in a great fair,' Rutherford preached. 'They go through the market and commend everything they see, but never open their purse to buy anything. So multitudes can say, "It is good to be a Christian. The Son of God is worth all the world," but they will never offer a penny for Christ's cause.'

Sadness dogged his efforts as he laboured to draw his congregation to Christ: 'I have a grieved heart daily in my calling,' Rutherford said.

But he pressed on and trusted Christ for the salvation of their souls. 'Prize Christ and salvation above all the world,' he urged his flock. 'Without faith in Christ and repentance you cannot see God.'

'I would lay my dearest joys in the gap between you and eternal destruction,' he told them. 'Your heaven would be two heavens for me and the salvation of you all as two salvations for me.'

Rutherford led them to Christ and also prepared them for trials. 'Know therefore,' Rutherford preached, 'that this is a race of God's choosing and not of our own; and the ill roads, the deep waters, the sharp showers and the bitter violent winds that are in our face, are of God's disposing. We will not get a better road than our Lord allows us. He has called us to suffering, and not a stone is in our way by chance.'

He poured his lifeblood into shepherding his flock. At the close of most Lord's Days after preaching the evening service, he experienced exhaustion and chest pains. His diligent labours became legendary. One man said of him, 'He is always praying, always preaching, always visiting the sick, always teaching, always writing and studying.'

One pastor who observed Rutherford's ministry said, 'I have known many great and good ministers in this church, but for such a piece of clay as Mr Rutherford was, I never knew one in Scotland like him, to whom so many great gifts were given.'

Through the years, many in his congregation believed in Jesus, and Christ transformed their lives. John Livingstone said of Rutherford, 'While he was at Anwoth, he was the instrument of much good among the poor ignorant people, many of which he brought to the knowledge and practice of religion.'

Before long, Rutherford's preaching became known throughout Galloway. Rich and poor from all around the region crowded into the Anwoth sanctuary to hear him. One minister said, 'He was a great strengthener of all the Christians in that country.'

Another man observed: 'The whole country indeed were to him, and accounted themselves, as his particular flock.'

As his fame spread, people came from great distances to hear Rutherford preach. Many visitors spent the night in his home and ate a meal at his table. The story of a visit to Anwoth by the celebrated Protestant bishop of the Church of Ireland, James Ussher, became widely known. Some have doubted the authenticity of the story. However, Ussher did make frequent visits from Ireland to England. A common route went from Ireland by ship to south-west Scotland and then overland to England. His travels would have led him down the road which passed near the front gate of Rutherford's manse, and it seems likely that he would have turned in to visit the famous pastor.

As the story goes, one Saturday evening, a lone traveller knocked on Rutherford's door. 'May I lodge here for the night?' the man asked.

Rutherford welcomed him gladly and urged him to warm himself by the fire. After supper, he asked the stranger to join them for evening devotions. He read the Bible and members of the family took turns in prayer. Then Rutherford asked the children and adults questions about the Bible. He looked at the visitor and said, 'Good sir, how many commandments are there?'

'Eleven,' the stranger answered.

'Eleven?' repeated Rutherford in surprise.

'Yes — eleven,' the man replied.

Rutherford told him that there were Ten Commandments. However, the stranger remained convinced that the number was eleven. Soon they all retired for the night. Rutherford went to bed astonished at the man's lack of Bible knowledge.

Early Sunday morning, Rutherford went outside to pray. As he walked the path between his house and the church, he heard a man's voice. He looked around and saw the stranger, kneeling beneath a tree, pouring out his heart to God and asking a blessing for all who would come to worship that day. His fervent and thoughtful prayer impressed Rutherford deeply.

When the man rose from his knees, Rutherford approached him. 'Are you a minister?' he asked.

'I am indeed,' the man replied. 'I am James Ussher.'

Rutherford knew his name well. Ussher was a bishop in the Protestant Church of Ireland, widely admired as one of the most learned and holy men of the day. Ussher explained that he was passing through the area and had hoped to meet Rutherford and hear him preach. The two men warmly embraced and encouraged one another in the Lord.

'Would you be willing to preach at Anwoth this morning?' Rutherford asked.

Ussher accepted the offer. When he entered the pulpit, he read the Bible passage for his sermon: 'A new commandment I give unto you, that ye love one another.' Rutherford smiled and said to himself, 'Aye, there is the Eleventh Commandment.'

Rutherford did not let his growing popularity go to his head — he knew his own heart too well. 'I have seen my abominable vileness,' he confessed to a friend. 'If I were well known, there would be none in this kingdom to ask how I do.'

Yet the sense of his own sin did not lead to despair because he relied wholeheartedly in his union with Christ. 'O sweet word!' Rutherford exclaimed. 'I live no more, but Christ lives in me!'

'Alas! I have little of Him! Yet I long for more,' he wrote. 'I am in every way as hard-headed and dead as any man, but yet I speak to Christ through my sleep.'

Rutherford believed that the sovereign Lord had chosen him for Anwoth. In a letter to a friend he wrote: 'The great master-gardener, the Father of our Lord Jesus Christ, in a wonderful providence, planted me here, where, by His grace, in this part of His vineyard I grow.'

As Rutherford's reputation spread, he received invitations to preach throughout Scotland, but he was determined to stay at home and shepherd his flock. 'I do not stir beyond the parish,' he said.

In Rutherford's day, the Church of Scotland celebrated the Lord's Supper infrequently. Most congregations hosted a communion service just twice a year. They often joined with surrounding parishes, leading to several hundred communicants. Samuel Rutherford believed that Christ met his children in a special way in the Lord's Supper. To him the sacrament was not just a remembrance of Christ's sacrifice, but a meal that believers enjoy with their Saviour. He described communion as a time 'wherein our well-beloved Jesus rejoices and is merry with His friends.'

Following the pattern of the Scottish Kirk, Rutherford preached a sermon of preparation on the Saturday evening before a Sunday communion service. He used these occasions to lift high the cross of Christ, teaching that by eating and drinking the Lord's Supper by faith, Christians proclaimed before men that 'Christ is our slain Redeemer.'

At Anwoth, the oak communion table, covered with a white linen cloth, was surrounded by chairs. The participants came in groups and sat around the table. Rutherford gave a short exhortation to each group of communicants as they took their turn eating the bread and drinking the wine at the table. Communion services lasted many hours, beginning early in the morning and continuing until late in the afternoon. Rutherford found rich personal blessings in the Lord's Supper. 'The timber and stones of the church-wall shall bear witness,' he told his flock, 'that my soul was refreshed in the comforts of God in that supper!'

In the midst of the joys of his flourishing ministry at Anwoth, sorrow often gripped his life. He and Eupham had two children but they both died in infancy. Then his wife, whom he called 'the delight of my eyes', suffered a long and painful illness. 'She is sorely tormented night and day,' he wrote. 'She can't sleep, and she cries like a woman travailing in birth.'

Caring for his invalid wife and watching her agony exacted an immense toll on Rutherford. 'I am so comfortless and so full of heaviness,' he informed a friend, 'that I am not able to stand under the burden any longer — my life is bitter to me and I fear the Lord to be my adversary.'

After nursing her through many weeks of suffering, he wrote: 'My wife is still in exceeding great pain at night and day. Pray for us, for my life was never so worrisome to me. God has filled me with gall and wormwood.'

In 1630, after thirteen months of agony, Eupham died, leaving Rutherford heart-stricken and alone. However, like

Job, he accepted this dark providence from God. 'The Lord has done it,' he wrote, 'blessed be His name.'

In the midst of his wife's illness, Rutherford himself suffered a debilitating, three-month sickness with high fevers and exhaustion. Even after the illness subsided, Rutherford reported that he could preach 'but once on the Sabbath with great difficulty'. It broke his heart that he was unable to visit his flock for months. 'An afflicted life looks very like the way that leads to the kingdom,' he said.

His widowed mother came to live with him after his wife died. But soon her fragile health broke down. 'God, knowing my present state, and the necessities of my calling,' Rutherford told a friend, 'I hope will spare my mother's life for a time.'

'It is, I know,' he wrote, 'hard to keep sight of God in a storm.'

But God chose not to spare his mother. 'My mother is weak, and I think shall leave me alone,' he wrote a friend, 'but I am not alone, because Christ's Father is with me.'

A few weeks later, she died. Through his grief he clung to God. 'Welcome, cross of Christ, if Christ be with it,' he professed. 'I know of no tree that bears sweeter fruit than Christ's cross.'

Sorrows made him long for heaven. 'I am a man often borne down and hungry,' he said, 'and waiting for the marriage supper of the Lamb.'

Rutherford knew that God used difficulties for the good of his children to teach them valuable lessons. He strove to find God's gifts hidden in his trials. 'When I am in the cellar of affliction,' he wrote, 'I look for the Lord's choicest wines.'

While enduring so much family loss and sorrow, he found comfort in visits from his brother George, a schoolteacher in nearby Kirkcudbright.

Rutherford employed all that he had learned through his suffering to comfort and counsel others. From the depth of his own experience, he offered advice to parents on the death of their children. 'Let your children be as so many flowers, borrowed from God,' Rutherford wrote to a mother after her daughter died. 'If the flowers die or wither, thank God for a summer loan of them and keep on the most intimate terms with Him.'

Three separate times he sent words of consolation to Lady Kenmure following the death of one of her children. When her daughter passed away, he wrote: 'What she wanted of time, that she has gotten in eternity.'

He knew it to be the Christian's duty to respond to trial and loss with a hearty faith in God. 'Faith will teach you to kiss a striking Lord,' he wrote Lady Kenmure, 'and so acknowledge the sovereignty of God in the death of a child to be above the power of us mortal men ... If our dear Lord pluck up one of His roses, and pull down sour and green fruit before harvest, who can challenge Him?'

'We do not take it ill if our children outrun us in the life of grace,' he wrote a bereaved parent. 'Why, then, are we sad, if they outstrip us in the attainment of the life of glory? It would seem that there is more reason to grieve that children lived after us, than that they are glorified and died before.'

'There is no way of quieting the mind and silencing the heart of a mother on the loss of her child, but godly submission,' Rutherford said.

To everyone undergoing trials he advised, 'Consider what the Lord is doing in it.'

But all the time Rutherford was caring for his flock, Charles I was plotting to force the Church of Scotland to do his bidding regarding worship and the administration of the Kirk. The king's designs would eventually lead to Samuel Rutherford's arrest and banishment from Anwoth.

3

Trial

'And the high priest questioned them, saying, "We strictly charged you not to teach in this name, yet here you have filled Jerusalem with your teaching..." But Peter and the apostles answered, "We must obey God rather than men"'
(Acts 5:27-29).

Rutherford was a thoroughgoing Reformed Presbyterian who cherished the doctrines of the *Scots Confession of 1560* and the Reformed creeds of the Continent. Although the pastor of an isolated rural flock, Rutherford kept his pulse on the politics of the kingdom, maintaining regular correspondence with Presbyterian ministers and nobles in Edinburgh and other Scottish towns. For this, Anwoth proved to be strategically important. It was the parish of Lord Gordon, the most influential nobleman in the region. Also, Anwoth lay in the heart of south-west Scotland, the strongest area for Presbyterianism in the land; and the highway linking England and Ireland ran right through the parish. When Charles I began to take bolder steps to force high-church episcopacy on all his subjects, Rutherford, and many others with him, grew very alarmed.

King Charles and Bishop of London William Laud — later to become Archbishop of Canterbury who served as the king's right-hand man for church affairs — decided to make an example of Alexander Leighton. Dr Leighton was a Scottish Presbyterian minister and a physician teaching at the college of physicians in London. Leighton wrote a book against episcopacy which referred to the king respectfully, but labelled the bishops of the Church of England 'men of blood' and 'popish prelates'. This earned him the wrath of Laud. In June 1630, Laud hauled him before the Star Chamber, a secret court that denied defendants the right to present witnesses or appeal the verdict. The Star Chamber levied a sentence against him which outraged the entire kingdom. A hangman publicly whipped Leighton, cut off his ears, slit his nose, and used a burning iron to brand his cheeks with the initials S.S. for 'Sower of Sedition'. Unable to walk after the ordeal, guards dragged him back to the Fleet prison where he was cast into a cell to serve a life sentence.

While Leighton languished in prison, Rutherford wrote him a letter. 'One day in heaven will have paid you — yea, and overpaid your blood, bonds, sorrow, and sufferings. O, but your hourglass of sufferings and losses, comes to little when it shall be counted and compared with the glory that abides you on the other side of the water! I think you could wish for more ears to give than you have, since you hope these ears you now have given Him shall be passages to take in the music of His glorious voice ... I know your sufferings for

Him are your glory; and therefore, weary not. His salvation is near at hand and shall not tarry.'

Leighton's plight served as a dark harbinger for what lay ahead. 'Our prelates assure us,' Rutherford wrote a friend, 'that for such as will not conform, there is nothing but imprisonment and deprivation.'

In 1634, Bishop Lamb of Galloway died. Although Lamb did not support the defenders of Reformed Presbyterianism, he left alone good men like Rutherford who faithfully served their parishes. His successor, Thomas Sydserff, a proponent of the high-church ceremonies being pushed by King Charles on the Scottish church, exuded an altogether different spirit. Sydserff immediately launched a purge of nonconformists. If magistrates refused to implement his demands to remove ministers who would not conform to episcopacy, he ordered the magistrates to be arrested as well.

When Bishop Sydserff tried to force a minister on the church at Kirkcudbright against the will of the congregation, Rutherford urged the town's chief magistrate to resist. 'I would counsel you to write to Edinburgh to some lawyers,' he advised, 'to understand what the magistrate may do in opposing any intruded minister.'

As pressures mounted on the Presbyterians of the Church of Scotland, Rutherford felt compelled to mobilize all who would listen to resist. 'I dare not for my soul be silent,' he wrote in March 1634, 'to see my Lord's house burning, and not cry "Fire, fire!"'

To win over Scottish nobles to his policies, King Charles I lavished them with titles and lands. In 1633, he elevated John Gordon, the Presbyterian patron of Rutherford, to the title of Viscount Kenmure, which significantly expanded his estates. And Charles's favours did their work. Later, when Kenmure sat in Parliament in Edinburgh, he sacrificed his principles and refused to take a stand against the king's plan to force English episcopacy upon Scotland. Although he longed to see the Kirk free from the king's control, he lacked the courage to resist. Instead, he feigned sickness and escaped to his castle in Galloway.

A year later, Kenmure fell gravely ill. When Rutherford came to visit him, Kenmure told him: 'I never dreamed that death had such a terrible, austere and gloomy countenance. I dare not die; howbeit, I know I must die.'

Over the course of several days, Rutherford called him to repent and trust Christ for the forgiveness of his sins. Wracked by a guilty conscience, Kenmure confessed his cowardice. 'I have found the weight of the wrath of God for not giving testimony for the Lord my God when I had occasion once in my life at the last Parliament for which fault how fierce have I found the wrath of the Lord! My soul has raged and roared. I have been grieved at the remembrance of it.'

A relative asked Kenmure why he had brought Rutherford to Galloway in the first place. 'God knows,' he answered, 'that I rejoice that ever God did put it in my heart so to do; and now, because I aimed at God's glory in it, the Lord has made me to find comfort to my soul in the end. The ministers of

Galloway murdered my father's soul, and if this man had not come, they would have murdered mine also.'

Samuel Rutherford was at his bedside when he died. He reported that before Kenmure expired, he smiled joyfully with a glorious look on his face. 'And so he died sweetly and holily,' Rutherford wrote, 'and his end was peace.'

Several years later, in order to warn Presbyterian nobles against compromising the gospel, Rutherford wrote a tract entitled *The Last and Heavenly Speeches and Glorious Departure of John, Viscount Kenmure.*

In the midst of his many duties, Rutherford managed to write a scholarly book against the teachings of the Dutch theologian Jacobus Arminius. Arminius taught that salvation was not wholly a gift of God's free grace, but was dependent on man's free will. Rutherford disagreed. It was not man's will that leads to Christ, Rutherford taught, 'but grace, grace, free grace, the merits of Christ for nothing.' He wrote a book in defence of the biblical doctrine that God's sovereign grace alone is the basis of salvation. It was published in Amsterdam in 1636 to much acclaim in Western Europe and Britain, winning him a reputation as an outstanding Reformed theologian. The book enraged the Scottish bishops, many of whom were Arminians. It also won him the ire of Bishop Sydserff.

Sydserff summoned Rutherford and demanded that he conform to episcopacy and renounce Presbyterian worship and government. Rutherford steadfastly refused. 'Our prelate will have us to swallow our light and we should vomit our conscience in this troublesome conformity,' he wrote to Lady Kenmure. 'But we must either see all the evil of ceremonies to be as indifferent as straws or suffer no less than to be cast out of the Lord's inheritance.'

The Archbishop of St Andrews and the king had granted the bishop of each diocese in Scotland the power to convene a Court of High Commission with broad powers to throw ministers out of their churches and fine or imprison anyone who impeded the court's commands. The Bishop of Galloway seized some of Rutherford's personal papers that contained references to corruption in the hierarchy of the Church of Scotland. The papers, together with the bishop's complaint against Rutherford, were laid before King Charles. 'I hang by a thread,' Rutherford wrote a friend, 'but it is of Christ's spinning.'

He knew that his days in Anwoth were numbered. 'It has pleased the Lord to let me see, by all appearances,' Rutherford said, 'my labours in God's house here at an end, and I must now learn to suffer.'

In the spring of 1636, Sydserff ordered Rutherford before his court in Wigton and summarily removed him from his ministry in Anwoth. Wanting the sentence confirmed by a higher court and hoping that sterner measures would be taken against Rutherford — perhaps banishment to the plantations of the New World — Bishop Sydserff charged Rutherford to appear before the Court of High Commission in Edinburgh.

One morning in late July 1636, Samuel Rutherford closed the door to his manse, stepped onto the dirt road and began to walk the 100-mile journey to Edinburgh to be tried again for nonconformity. As he trod the narrow lane from Anwoth, members of his congregation came to bid him farewell. For nine years, he had preached to them in church and taught them in their fields and farmhouses. Tears streamed down the cheeks of shepherd boys and poor cottagers who could not bear to watch their minister thrown from his home and church. Several members of the congregation accompanied Rutherford to Edinburgh to support him as he stood trial.

When he arrived in Edinburgh, the Court of High Commission made up of bishops and noblemen, including Sydserff, tried his case for three days. The lead judge plied him with questions that had nothing to do with the charges against him. 'I wholly declined to answer,' Rutherford told a friend, 'notwithstanding his threats.'

The commission took umbrage at Rutherford's book against Arminianism and his unwillingness to conform to the worship ceremonies demanded by the king. His steadfast refusal to call the bishops 'lord' added fuel to the fire of their indignation.

A Highland noble spoke in support of Rutherford and even a few bishops defended him. When Sydserff began to fear that the commission might be lenient with him, he swore with an oath that if they did not deal sternly with Rutherford, he would bring the matter directly to the king.

Sydserff need not have worried. The court confirmed the expulsion of Rutherford from his pastoral ministry, forbade him to preach anywhere in Scotland and banished him to Aberdeen, a city 200 miles to the north. Rutherford submitted to God's will. After the sentence was pronounced, he turned to a friend and said, 'There is no quarrel more honest or honourable than to suffer for truth. That honour my kind Lord has now bestowed upon me, even to suffer for my royal and princely King Jesus. I go to my King's palace at Aberdeen. Tongue, pen, and wit can not express my joy!'

The court refused to allow him adequate time to return to Anwoth to collect his things and say goodbye. He had to set out for Aberdeen at once. 'My Lord ruled it, so I am filled with joy in my sufferings,' he said, 'and I find Christ's cross sweet.'

Although things appeared dark for the church in Scotland, Rutherford looked to the future with confidence. 'Doubt not, fear not,' he wrote a friend. 'They shall not, who now ride highest, put Christ out of His kingly possession in Scotland.'

4

Exile

'Woe to me if I do not preach the gospel!'
(1 Corinthians 9:16).

A few members of Rutherford's Anwoth congregation travelled with him all the way to Aberdeen, the grey windswept city on the North Sea. He stopped in Irvine to visit the celebrated minister David Dickson whose support buoyed his spirits. Throughout his northward journey, Rutherford reported that he experienced kindness from nearly everyone. 'All men I look in the face — of whatever denomination, nobles and poor, acquaintances and strangers — are friendly to me,' he said.

Rutherford's enemies had selected Aberdeen for his banishment for two reasons: it was far removed from Galloway and Edinburgh where Rutherford had influence, and more of its clergy had embraced episcopacy than in any other Scottish city. He took up residence in a rented room on Upperkirkgate Street in the town's centre. The Court of High Commission had forbidden him under pain of rebellion from leaving Aberdeen or preaching without the king's permission. But they did not place him under house arrest; he was free to move about the city.

In contrast to the encouragement given him during his trek into exile, Rutherford received a cool reception from the citizens of Aberdeen. 'Many think me a strange man and my cause not good,' he wrote a friend.

As he walked the streets, he heard himself referred to as 'the banished minister'. 'I am not ashamed of my garland,' Rutherford informed a friend.

He called himself 'the Lord's prisoner'. Some people were kind to him, he admitted, but 'in the night under their breath'. Even the ministers in the city who favoured Presbyterianism failed to associate with him publicly. 'It is counted wisdom by most not to countenance a confined minister,' Rutherford reported.

Soon the absence from his church weighed heavily upon his heart. 'Fair, fair Anwoth,' he often sighed. Isolated and alone, Rutherford turned to letter-writing as his only means of contact with his flock and his friends in the south. 'I think,' he wrote a member of his congregation, 'the sparrows and swallows that build their nests at Anwoth blessed birds.'

Rutherford chafed under the preaching ban and called it 'my greatest grief'. To a friend in Galloway, he described preaching as his 'one good eye'. 'I had but one eye, and they have put it out,' Rutherford wrote. 'My one joy, next to the flower of my joys, Christ, was to preach my sweetest,

sweetest Master and the glory of His kingdom; and it seemed no cruelty to them to put out the poor man's one eye.'

'My dumb Sabbaths burden my heart,' Rutherford wrote, 'they are like a stone tied to a bird's foot.'

Despite the judgement of the High Commission, Rutherford believed that legally and in the eyes of God, he remained the minister of Anwoth parish. His congregation felt the same. Concern for his flock drove him to write frequently, inquiring of their spiritual welfare and encouraging them in their faith. 'O! How rich a prisoner were I,' he communicated to Anwoth, 'if I could obtain of the Lord the salvation of you all.'

To one Anwoth congregant he wrote: 'I long exceedingly to know if the oft spoken of match between you and Christ holds; and if you follow on to know the Lord. Next to my Lord Jesus, and his fallen Kirk, you have the greatest share of my sorrow, and also of my joy.'

'I cannot tell what is become of my labours among that people,' he wrote to a minister whose parish adjoined Anwoth. 'If all that my Lord has built by me be cast down, and the bottom fall out of the profession of that parish, and none stand by Christ, whose love I once preached as clearly and plainly as I could ... How can I bear it?'

Shortly after Rutherford began his exile in Aberdeen, Bishop Sydserff arrested his brother, George Rutherford, for his Presbyterian convictions and his close association with Samuel. The bishop's court removed George from his post as schoolmaster in Kirkcudbright and expelled him from the town. Later, when Samuel learned that George had moved to Ayrshire — a county in south-west Scotland — he wrote to Lord Loudoun, the leading Presbyterian nobleman in the area: 'Please befriend my brother, now suffering for the same cause; for as he is to dwell nigh your Lordship's bounds, your Lordship's word and countenance may help him.'

Sometimes Rutherford chided himself for his failures as a pastor, confessing his 'daily sorrow' from the memory of 'my neglects while I had a pulpit.' At other times, he defended his ministry. 'I am free from the blood of all men,' Rutherford wrote to his Anwoth parishioners, 'for I ceased not, while I was among you, in season and out of season, according to the measure of grace given unto me, to warn and stir up your minds … for I have communicated to you the whole counsel of God.'

Rutherford asked friends to undertake a letter-writing campaign to convince Presbyterian nobles throughout Scotland to petition the High Commission for his release and return to Anwoth. 'I would that honest and lawful means were essayed for bringing me home to my charge,' he wrote a friend. 'As for liberty, without I be restored to my flock, it is little to me, for my silence is my greatest prison.'

In an effort to discredit Rutherford and the Presbyterian cause, the ministers of Aberdeen preached against him and his doctrine — sometimes while he sat in the congregation. The professors of divinity at Marischal College in Aberdeen, led by Robert Barron, staged three debates with Rutherford on theology and the high-church ceremonies being pressed upon the Church of Scotland. 'I am here troubled with disputes of the great doctors,' he wrote.

But Rutherford believed he got the better of the debates. 'Dr Barron has often disputed with me, especially about Arminian controversies and for the ceremonies,' he wrote. 'Three yokings laid him by; and I have not been troubled with him since.'

Although most of the townspeople's attitude toward Rutherford remained 'cold and dry', he was pleased to report, 'yet I find a lodging in the heart of many strangers'.

Some people in Aberdeen began to seek out Rutherford to talk with him. Before long, he started to see fruit from his conversations with them. A few even appealed to Edinburgh to set him free. 'There is some blossoming of Christ's kingdom in this town,' Rutherford informed a friend in Galloway, 'and the smoke is rising and the ministers are raging; but I like the rumbling and roaring devil best.'

When the local clergymen got wind of Rutherford's influence, they threatened his visitors with censures. Some of the city's pastors petitioned the authorities to have him banished further north. 'I find the ministers working for my confinement in Caithness and Orkney,' Rutherford wrote, 'because some people here, willing to be edified, resort to me.'

There was talk that Rutherford would be exiled from Britain altogether. 'Banishment out of the kingdom,' Rutherford informed a friend, 'is determined against me, as I hear this land is not able to bear me.'

In the midst of the loneliness and isolation of his exile in Aberdeen, Rutherford vacillated between spiritual highs and lows. Often, he exalted in his Saviour, grateful to be persecuted for his cause. 'It is for God's truth and the honour of my King and royal prince Jesus, I now suffer', he wrote, 'and howbeit this town is my prison, yet Christ has made it my palace, a garden of pleasures, a field and orchard of delight.'

'I would not exchange my prison and sad nights', Rutherford wrote, 'with the court, honour, and ease of my adversaries: my Lord visits my soul with feasts of spiritual comfort.'

'I never knew', he revealed to Lady Kenmure, 'by my nine years' preaching so much of Christ's love as He has taught me in Aberdeen by six months imprisonment.'

In another letter, he remarked that he felt so near to Christ that 'all before was but childhood and bairn's play'.

But on days when the dark clouds of his circumstances overwhelmed him, especially the preaching ban, he saw things quite differently. To a friend he described himself as 'weeping in prison'. In one letter he confessed: 'By reason of my silence, sorrow, sorrow hath filled me. My harp is hanged up on the willow trees, because I am in a strange land.'

Fears of even greater trials in the future haunted him. 'I go halting and sighing', he confided, 'fearing there be an unseen process yet coming out and that heavier than I can answer.'

At times, he accused God of treating him unfairly. 'I took up an action against Christ,' he confessed to a nobleman, 'and brought a plea against His love, and libelled unkindness against Christ my Lord, and I said, "This is my death; He has forgotten me."'

Once he complained that God was 'seeking to take down my sails like an old broken ship let to lie on the coast that is no more for the sea'.

Believers of Rutherford's age called this absence of the Lord's presence being 'under desertion'. But Rutherford always came around to a realization of God's love. 'Patient submission to God under desertion is sweet,' Rutherford said.

To a minister friend he confided: 'When I look over beyond the line, and beyond death, to the laughing side of the world, I triumph and ride upon the high places of Jacob; howbeit otherwise I am a faint, dead-hearted, cowardly man, oft borne down, and hungry and waiting for the marriage supper of the Lamb. Nevertheless, I think it is the Lord's wise love that feeds us with hunger, and makes us fat with wants and desertions.'

'How sad a prisoner should I be if I knew not that my Lord Jesus had the keys of the prison himself,' he noted. 'There is no sweeter fellowship with Christ than to bring our wounds and our sores to him.'

As he grew less hopeful of being allowed to minister publicly in Scotland again, he considered going to New England or the Continent, if ever he was released from confinement. But knowing God's sovereign hand was active in all his circumstances comforted him. 'I bless the Lord that all our troubles come through Christ's fingers,' he wrote.

His relationship with Christ sustained him: 'My Lord Jesus has fully recompensed my sadness with His joys, my losses with His own presence. I find it a sweet and rich thing to exchange my sorrows with Christ's joys, my afflictions for that sweet peace I have with Him.'

Although Samuel Rutherford knew that every Christian's relationship with the Lord should have a strong emotional element, he warned believers not to put too much stock in the ups and downs of their feelings. 'Believe Christ's love more than your own feelings,' he advised a parishioner. 'Your Rock does not ebb and flow, though your sea does.'

To another he wrote: 'Your heart is not the compass that Christ sails by.'

Throughout his exile, he prayed that God would restore him to his calling. 'O, if I might but speak to three or four herdboys of my worthy Master,' he wrote, 'I would be satisfied to be the meanest and most obscure of all the pastors in this land and to live in any place, in any of Christ's basest outhouses!'

While enduring the preaching ban, Rutherford put his pen to work as his pulpit. He wrote to encourage and challenge his congregation hidden in the hills of Galloway. His letters throbbed with pathos and overflowed with biblical imagery. He warned backsliders, comforted the grieving, counselled young men and prepared his readers for coming trials. And always, as he had done in his sermons, he pointed his flock to Christ and their heavenly home.

'O if you saw the beauty of Jesus,' he wrote, 'and smelled the fragrance of His love, you would run through fire and water to be at Him.'

In one letter he said, 'If there were 10,000 thousand millions of worlds, and as many heavens, full of men and angels, Christ would not be pinched to supply all our wants and to fill us all. Christ is a well of life; but who knows how deep it is to the bottom?'

Through his letters, he implored his flock and friends to cling to the Saviour and strive for holiness: 'Hold fast Christ without wavering and contend for the faith because Christ is not easily gotten nor kept.'

He reminded them that their sanctification, although the work of God's grace, called for self-denial and diligence. 'Therefore dig deep,' he counselled, 'and sweat and labour and take pains for Him, and set by as much time in the day for Him as you can. He will be won with labour.'

At the bottom of the hard work of sanctification, Rutherford assured them, was Christ at work in them. He encouraged them to say, 'It is not I, but Christ; not I, but grace; not I, but God's glory; not I, but God's love constraining me; not I, but the Lord's Word; not I, but Christ's commandin me!'

And Rutherford warned that those who live for themselves and not for God will bitterly regret it in the end. 'Take pains for your salvation,' he wrote, 'for in that day when you shall see many men's labours and acquisitions and idol riches lying in ashes, when the earth and all the works thereof shall be burned with fire, O how dear a price would your soul give for God's favour in Christ!'

He had a gift for showing people an eternal perspective. 'Look beyond time,' he advised. 'Things here are but moonshine; they have but children's wit who are delighted with shadows and diluted with feathers flying in the air.'

'This life is nothing in comparison of eternity,' Rutherford proclaimed.

Confident that the trials that believers endure are orchestrated by God for their good, Rutherford strove to instil in his flock a Christ-centred view of suffering. 'Four and twenty hours' abode in heaven is worth three score and ten years' sorrow upon earth,' he wrote.

'And for no other cause,' Rutherford counselled, 'does the Lord withdraw from you the childish toys and the earthly delights that He gives unto others, but that He may have you wholly to Himself.'

To a woman facing difficult circumstances he wrote: 'Think it not hard if you get not your will, nor your delights in this life; God will have you to rejoice in nothing but Him.'

'Grace grows best in winter,' he wrote.

'O what owe I to the file, to the hammer, to the furnace of my Lord Jesus!' Rutherford proclaimed. 'Grace tried is better than grace, and it is more than grace. It is glory in its infancy. Who knows the truth of grace without a trial? And how soon would faith freeze without a cross!'

All of life's sufferings would be worth it in the end, Rutherford assured his people. 'Travelling to heaven is a well-spent journey, even though seven deaths lay between.'

In fact, Rutherford believed that God brought to his children just the amount of suffering they needed to fit them for heaven. 'Madam,' he wrote to Lady Kenmure, 'when you are come to the other side of the water, and have set down your foot on the shore of glorious eternity, and look back again to the waters and to your wearisome journey, and see in that clear glass of endless glory, nearer to the bottom of God's wisdom, you shall then be forced to say, "If God had done otherwise with me than He has done, I would have never come to the enjoying of this crown of glory."'

Rutherford's letters brought consolation to the lord in his castle and the peasant farmer at his plough, to the troubled lady in her manor house and the widow in her cottage. His letters proved to be such a source of encouragement and instruction to the recipients that many began to circulate them among their friends.

Although he wrote hundreds of letters from his exile in Aberdeen, his flock did not always write back. 'I complain that Galloway is not kind to me in paper,' he wrote. 'I have received but two letters in sixteen weeks ... I wish that my friends in Galloway forget me not.'

To keep abreast with the struggle between king and Kirk, Rutherford maintained regular communication with leading Presbyterian ministers like Alexander Henderson and David Dickson. These ministers would soon direct the efforts to restore Reformed Presbyterianism to the Scottish church. Rutherford, with other like-minded men, worked to embolden pastors and the Scottish nobility to defend the Presbyterian Kirk. 'Duties are ours,' Rutherford wrote to Dickson, 'events are the Lord's.'

He used stark language to stir up his brothers in the struggle. To John Nevay, the Presbyterian pastor in Newmilns, he wrote: 'I am not a little grieved that our mother church is running so quickly to the brothel-house, and that we are hiring lovers and giving gifts to the Great Mother of Fornications. Alas, that our Husband is like to quit us so shortly ... take hold of Him and keep Him in this land.'

Because Rutherford believed that nobles would play a vital role in defending the liberty of the Church of Scotland, he addressed many of his letters to them. He also knew that riches, status, lands and power posed powerful temptations to hold them back. 'Worldly glory is nothing but a vapour, a shadow, the foam of the water, or something less and lighter — even nothing,' Rutherford reminded a noblewoman.

'Now He is asking if your Lordship will help Him against the mighty of the earth,' Rutherford wrote to the Earl of Cassilis, 'when men are setting their shoulders to Christ's fair and beautiful tent in this land to loosen its stakes and break it down... Back Christ now, when so many think it wisdom to let Him to fend for Himself.'

'They are not worthy of Jesus who will not take a blow for their Master's sake,' Rutherford proclaimed.

To Lord Loudoun he advised: 'You are many ways blessed of God, who have taken upon you to come out to the streets with Christ on your forehead, when so many are ashamed of Him... Go on in the strength of the Lord and keep Christ, avouch Him that He may read your name publicly before men and angels.'

Keeping an eye on eternity, Rutherford counselled nobles on what was their wisest course. 'Kneel to Christ and kiss the Son,' he wrote. 'There will be shortly a proclamation by the One standing in the clouds that time shall be no more and that courts with kings of clay shall be no more and prisons, confinements, forfeitures of nobles, wrath of kings, hazard of lands, houses and name for Christ shall be no more.'

While he languished in exile in Aberdeen, Presbyterians in Edinburgh and throughout the land grew more resistant to the changes being forced on the Kirk by Charles and Laud. Back in 1634, Charles had ordered four Scottish bishops, including Sydserff of Galloway and the Bishop of Aberdeen, to compile a book of canons for the Church of Scotland. By 1635, they had completed the work and submitted it to Archbishop Laud. After further revision by English prelates, the canons received royal approval.

The manner in which the book of canons had been formed and adopted had violated the constitutional principles of the Church of Scotland. Since the Reformation, the General Assembly was the highest church authority, but it had never been consulted about the canons. They were written and approved by royal authority alone.

Far worse than that, the canons prescribed foreign ceremonies, prayers and practices contrary to the Kirk's understanding of the Scriptures. The canons gave bishops great power and forbade private meetings to teach the Bible without approval of the bishop. The canons also required the use of Laud's edition of the *Book of Common Prayer,* which added more ritual than earlier versions and included new phrasing taken nearly word for word from the Roman Catholic Mass book. The set prayers and rituals of what the Scots called 'Laud's Liturgy' were a far cry from the unadorned worship, informed by the Scriptures, that Scottish Presbyterians had offered to God since the Reformation. In addition, once the prayer book was implemented, Scottish ministers were to be banned from praying extemporaneously in church.

Rutherford abhorred the unbiblical demands made by Laud's Liturgy, including that communion should be received according to the episcopal practice — kneeling at the front of the church. He saw kneeling to receive the elements as a throw-back to the Catholic adoration of the elements as containing the physical body and blood of Christ and called it 'idolatry'. There were those in the Church of Scotland who thought that making accommodations for some of the worship changes such as kneeling to receive the Lord's Supper was a small price to pay for harmony in the church.

Rutherford did not. 'The adoring of Christ by kneeling before bread and wine', he wrote his congregation from Aberdeen, 'should neither be permitted within the walls of Anwoth Kirk, nor practised by the people in any other place.'

Urging them to resist the episcopal ceremonies, he called them to follow 'the example of Christ our Lord, that is, that you should sit as banqueters at one table with our King and eat and drink and divide the elements, one to another.'

Meanwhile, Bishop Sydserff tried to force upon Anwoth a minister who embraced episcopal worship. When Rutherford got word of it, he warned his parishioners in stark terms against accepting any unbiblical practices. 'I counsel you to beware of the new strange leaven of men's inventions, besides and against the Word of God, contrary to the oath of this Kirk, now coming among you. Hate and keep yourselves from idols. Forebear in any case to hear the reading of the new fatherless service book, full of gross heresies, popish and superstitious errors without any warrant of Christ, tending to the overthrowing of preaching. You owe no allegiance to the bastard canons; they are unlawful, blasphemies and superstitions. The ceremonies that lie in Anti-Christ's foul womb, the wares of the great mother of fornications, the Kirk of Rome, are to be refused.'

Believing that Christ had entitled each church to consent to any minister chosen to lead them, the Anwoth congregation refused to accept the bishop's man. His flock's principled stand against the bishop's minister heartened Rutherford, but still he worried what would become of them, languishing without a faithful pastor. 'O, how my soul will mourn in secret,' he wrote, 'if my nine years' pained head and aching breast and pained back and grieved heart and private and public prayers to God will all be for nothing among that people!'

From all across Scotland, ministers and noblemen opposed Laud's prayer book and petitioned the king to permit them to worship as their consciences dictated. But this merely hardened Charles's resolve to have the Scots bow to his will — even in their worship of God. The prelates decreed that the *Book of Common Prayer* was to be used first in Edinburgh in the hope that it would set an example of acceptance to be followed throughout the country.

On Sunday morning, 23 July 1637, a tense crowd packed St Giles Kirk in Edinburgh. Wealthy noblemen and the poorest of the poor thronged the church. This was the day designated for the first use of the new prayer book in the capital city. The Bishop of Edinburgh and the Archbishop of St Andrews came to St Giles that morning to ensure that all went smoothly when the prayer book was introduced in the most influential church in Scotland. When a minister stood in the pulpit and began to read the opening prayer, the congregation began to murmur in protest. Soon an outcry arose from every corner of the building. The clamour spilled out onto the streets. All over Edinburgh, people protested the king's control of the church. The unrest spread to nearly every town and village in the land, as the pent-up frustrations of thirty years of interference from the Crown boiled over.

The king's Privy Council in Edinburgh saw the folly of forcing the worship book on the people and took steps to defuse the explosive situation. They sent word to the king in London, urging him to let the Scots worship as they pleased. Although the Scottish Privy Council, taking the pulse of the people, wanted to compromise, Charles did not. The king declared that anyone who refused to submit to his mandate regarding worship would be branded as rebels. 'I will rather die,' Charles said, 'than yield to those impertinent and damnable demands.'

Alarmed that the king's orders stripped them of any legal recourse, the Scots decided to make a National Covenant like their forbearers had done at the time of the Reformation. On a chilly February day in 1638, more than a thousand Scottish ministers and laymen streamed into Greyfriars Kirk in Edinburgh to adopt the National Covenant and break the king's domination over the church. The Covenant included the primary beliefs of the Church of Scotland and the errors that they stood against. It promised to honour and defend the king, but resist anything imposed on the church.

Hundreds signed the National Covenant that day, knowing that defying the king could cost them their lives. Couriers rushed copies of the Covenant to the four corners of the realm. All who supported the National Covenant were called Covenanters. After hearing how quickly the Scottish people embraced the National Covenant, the Archbishop of St Andrews said, 'Now all that we have been doing these thirty years past is thrown down at once.'

Shortly after the National Covenant began to circulate, Rutherford left Aberdeen without royal approval. Arriving in Edinburgh, he found the capital aflame with zeal to protect the Scottish Kirk and resist, with force of arms if necessary, the usurpations of the king. The leading Covenanter ministers in Edinburgh asked Rutherford to preach. Speaking to large gatherings of people of every rank in the college halls of the university and in the churches of the city, he called them to trust Christ and protect his Kirk. Afterward, Robert Baillie, a prominent Presbyterian minister, said, 'Mr Rutherford has an excellent gift, both of preaching and prayer. He fells all the bishops, and houghs [hamstrings] the ceremonies.'

In July 1638, after a two-year absence from his church, Rutherford was back preaching to his beloved congregation in Anwoth. The enthusiasm of the people for the National Covenant prevented the bishop from doing anything about it. Rutherford's prayer from Aberdeen had been answered: 'O, that my Lord would bring me among them, that I might tell uncommon and great tales of Christ to them.'

His flock rejoiced at his return for they were without a minister for nearly two years. Since he was exiled, 'No sound of the Word of God was heard,' they reported.

However, his return to Anwoth would not last long.

5

St Andrews

*'Put not your trust in princes, in a son of man,
in whom there is no salvation'*
(Psalm 146:3).

King Charles I insisted that the General Assembly of the Church of Scotland needed his permission to meet. The Scots were determined to call a General Assembly with or without Charles's consent. The king, aware of the Scots' united resistance to the prayer book and realizing they would meet anyway, granted permission and sent his commissioner, the Duke of Hamilton, to observe the proceedings and speak on his behalf.

In December 1638, the leaders of the Church of Scotland gathered in the High Kirk of Glasgow to hold their first General Assembly since King James had imposed the rule of bishops twenty years before. Rutherford attended as a delegate from the Presbytery of Kirkcudbright. The General Assembly sought to make clear that Christ alone was the Head of the Scottish church. The Scottish bishops refused to attend, but sent a formal protest, stating that the assembly was illegal and should be dismissed. The assembly rejected the protest and proceeded to bring charges against the bishops. Hamilton, the king's commissioner, said, 'If you pretend to assume the right to try the bishops, then I can neither give my consent nor witness it.'

The Reverend Alexander Henderson, the moderator, turned to Hamilton and said, 'We are his Majesty's true and loyal subjects and we acknowledge before God our obligation to give obedience to our king. But let God, by whom kings reign, have His own place. Let Christ Jesus, the King of kings, have His own way, by whose grace our king reigns.'

Hamilton responded by declaring the assembly dissolved and warning them not to continue their deliberations on pain of treason. Disregarding the objections and threats of the king's commissioner, the assembly pressed on. 'The church had a right from God,' the assembly asserted, 'which the prince could not in law or reason take from us to keep a General Assembly.'

The assembly appointed several committees to evaluate every aspect of the life and work of the church. Rutherford was appointed to a committee examining the liturgy, *Book of Canons* and the Court of High Commission. In short order, the assembly abolished the Court of High Commission and the *Book of Canons* and the *Prayer Book*. They argued that the king's imposition of episcopacy upon the Church of Scotland was unconstitutional and a violation of the National Covenant of 1580. Therefore, the assembly removed the bishops from office and reestablished a purely Presbyterian government, including the right of ruling elders to serve in the courts of the church, ridding the Church of Scotland of all that Charles and his father had forced upon her.

To end the despised practice of clergymen taking incomes from churches without ever setting foot in the parish, the assembly required ministers to reside in their parishes and preach regularly. They called for the building of church schools throughout Scotland. And they mandated the General Assembly to give careful oversight of the colleges of the land. Soon, the sweeping changes wrought by the Glasgow Assembly became known as the 'Second Reformation'.

Everyone at the General Assembly knew that this was not the end of their challenges, but the beginning. 'The wind is now on Christ's face in this land,' Rutherford wrote to Alexander Henderson, 'and seeing you are with Him you cannot expect the leeside, or the sunny side of the brae.'

The assembly asked the Scottish Privy Council to pass a law requiring every adult in the country to sign the National Covenant. At that time, the leaders of both church and state on all sides of the controversy thought that the unity, peace and blessing of the nation depended on religious uniformity. Religious toleration would be years in coming.

The General Assembly empowered a commission to advance the Presbyterian cause in the Church of Scotland by placing ministers of eminent talents and graces in strategic positions. Samuel Rutherford's writings had set him apart as a formidable scholar and champion of

Reformed Presbyterianism. The commission, convinced
that Rutherford's academic and spiritual gifts should not
be hidden away in a small country parish in Galloway,
appointed him to the vacant chair of theology at St Mary's
College, one of the colleges of St Andrews University. They
wanted Rutherford to train young men to be pastors.

Wanting desperately to remain with his flock at Anwoth,
Rutherford raised objections to his appointment. He wrote
to the commission asking if it was right to transfer a minister
and bring sorrow upon a congregation 'who have been
partakers of the sufferings of their pastor, as living in bonds
with him and who have hazard their persons and estates to
oppose an intruder'.

Rutherford protested that he had neither the 'gifts of mind'
nor strength of body to undertake such an important work.
He argued that to remove a minister from his flock without
the congregation's consent and 'impose on him the charge
of a doctor seems unlawful and most difficult'. In a humble
assessment of his ministry, he urged the commission not to
assign him a weightier responsibility when he felt unable in
his current office to 'be able to answer to Christ'.

The members of the Anwoth congregation petitioned the
commission. 'We most humbly intrigue your reverend and
godly wisdom in the bowels of Jesus Christ,' the parishioners
wrote, 'that you would not deprive us of such a comfortable
instrument wherewith the Lord has blessed us.' They
pleaded that the removal of their pastor would overwhelm
them with 'bitter grief'.

Nearly one hundred noblemen and ministers from across Galloway sent an appeal to the commission, protesting the decision to take Rutherford from their midst. 'God has blessed his labours in this country with a good success,' they stated. 'His removal will be a great discouragement to the ministers of the Presbytery of Kirkcudbright ... and the weakness of Mr Samuel's body requires a lesser charge than he has already. Seriously ponder what may be the consequences of grieving and discouraging such a considerable province as Galloway at such a time.'

Brushing aside the pleas of Rutherford, his congregants and his fellow presbyters, the commission directed Rutherford to report to St Andrews. However, he refused to comply with the commission before their recommendations had been formally approved by the General Assembly slated to meet in July of 1639. Rutherford and his flock hoped to convince the General Assembly to keep him at Anwoth.

'I must entreat you and your Christian acquaintances,' Rutherford wrote to a minister in Galloway, 'to remember me to God in your prayers and my flock and ministry and my transportation and removal from this place which I fear at this assembly.'

His commitment to his rural flock was remarkable since the call to occupy the chair of divinity at St Andrews University was one of the most prestigious posts in all of Scotland. Through it, Rutherford could wield great influence for the cause of Presbyterianism in the Kirk and mould the minds of her future leaders. When the General Assembly met, Rutherford argued that the assembly's commission had overstepped its authority by removing him without getting his consent or the consent of his congregation or presbytery. But his efforts were in vain. The delegates wanted him in St Andrews University, training the next generation. When Rutherford realized that he must yield to the assembly's request, he insisted that his call include preaching in a local congregation. He had had enough of 'silent Sabbaths' in Aberdeen. The General Assembly gladly appointed him to be an associate minister with Robert Blair who had been assigned to pastor a church in St Andrews.

St Andrews, having long been the seat of the archbishop, was a centre of support for episcopacy and Arminian theology. So Rutherford and Blair would face stiff opposition in the church and the university.

It must have been another tearful goodbye between Rutherford and his parishioners as he left Galloway to take up his new assignment. 'My removal from my flock is so heavy to me,' he wrote Lady Kenmure, 'that it makes my life a burden to me. I had never such a longing for death.'

In the late autumn of 1639, he arrived in St Andrews, the seaside town on Scotland's east coast. When he began his work at the university, it was in desperate need of reform. One student at the time said of St Andrews, 'The University of St Andrews was the very nursery of all superstition in worship and error in doctrine and the sink of all profanity in conversation among the students.'

Rutherford taught courses covering systematic theology, church history and Hebrew, and delivered series of lectures on books of the Bible. He had his work cut out for him to transform the college into a centre of biblically-based theological training. 'My desire', he said in describing his goals for St Mary's College, 'is that Christ may dwell in this society and that the youth may be fed with sound knowledge.'

From his earliest days of ministry, Rutherford had a heart for young people. At St Andrews, he relished the opportunity to deepen their love and knowledge of the Redeemer and his Word. 'O what a sweet couple, what a glorious yoke are youth and grace, Christ and a young man!' he said.

Knowing that young men faced many powerful temptations, he challenged them to hold fast to Jesus and fight the good fight. 'I entreat you now, in the morning of your life,' Rutherford once counselled a young man, 'to seek the Lord and His face. Beware of the folly of dangerous youth — a perilous time for your soul.'

Preparing them for the struggle against sin would not be easy. 'O, but pride of youth,' he taught, 'vanity, lust, idolizing of the world and charming pleasures take a long time to root out!'

Rutherford warned them that their warfare was not simply against their sinful desires. 'I recommend to you prayer and watching over the sins of your youth,' he advised, 'for I know that missive letters go between the devil and young blood. Satan has a friend at court in the heart of youth, and there pride, luxury, lust, revenge, forgetfulness of God are hired as his agents.'

Prayer, he knew, must be the students' lifeline if they would grow in grace. To Rutherford, prayer was a heartfelt conversation with God. One who knew him well said that often when Rutherford prayed, tears 'trickle down without intermission'. Throughout his life, he depended on the grace of God working through prayer, to keep him in the faith. Once, when he visited the manse of his friend James Guthrie in Stirling, a maid saw Rutherford walking alone in the house deep in prayer. She heard him say aloud, 'Lord, make me believe in Thee!' Then he sat down for a few minutes, got up and began to walk again and she overheard him say, 'Lord, make me love Thee!' Rutherford paused for a moment and then prayed again, 'Lord, make me keep all Thy commandments!'

In St Andrews, Rutherford did not enjoy the seclusion of a tree-lined glen for his morning prayer walks. He must have often strolled along the beach, praying for his students while gulls cried and waves lapped the shore. Perhaps he found a quiet place to pray near the martyr sites of the reformers Patrick Hamilton and George Wishart, who gave their lives for the Reformed faith before the Scottish Reformation.

His teaching, preaching and godly example soon had an effect. One of his students wrote that God so blessed Rutherford's ministry 'that the university forthwith became a Lebanon, out of which were taken cedars for building the house of the Lord through the whole land'.

Meanwhile, King Charles I, incensed by the independent spirit of the Church of Scotland's General Assembly, considered the Covenanters rebels. The king determined to put the Scots in their place by force of arms. When the Covenanters heard that Charles was organizing an army to invade Scotland, they prepared to defend themselves. Scottish noblemen from across the land rallied to the Covenanter cause, raising a 20,000-man force. The Scottish army was ably trained and led by experienced officers who had fought to protect Protestantism in Europe with Gustavus Adolphus.

Ministers preached daily to the Scottish troops and led them in worship. One eyewitness reported: 'Had you lent your ear in the morning, or especially at evening, and heard in the tents the sound of some singing psalms, some praying and some reading Scripture, you would have been refreshed.'

Another described the military units' patriotic zeal for Kirk and country. 'Every company had, flying at the captain's tent, a brave new colour, stamped with Scottish arms and the motto, "For Christ's Crown and Covenant", in golden letters.'

The Covenanter army captured several fortresses in the border region. When they clashed with the king's troops near Berwick, they forced them to retreat. This struggle came to be called the First Bishops' War. The Scots sent a communication to the king, expressing their loyalty, but insisting that Charles recognize the Scottish church's independence from the Crown.

In June 1639 the king, realizing that his poorly trained forces without the financial backing of the English Parliament could not defeat the Scots, signed a treaty to end hostilities with the Covenanters. Charles agreed to permit a General Assembly to meet that summer in Edinburgh. But Charles was simply buying time, scheming to raise a formidable army to crush the rebellious Scots as soon as possible. This began years of deceit and broken promises as Charles struggled to control the English Parliament and the Scots. One moment he told the Scots they could run the Church of Scotland as they pleased, and the next he threatened to invade.

If Charles hoped that the next General Assembly would be more agreeable to his will, he was sorely mistaken. The Edinburgh assembly ratified all the actions of the Glasgow assembly and sent them to the Scottish Parliament for its consent. Before Parliament could respond, Charles dissolved it. In June 1640, defying the king's command, the Scottish Parliament met without royal sanction and ratified all the decisions of the General Assembly, knowing that such a step would likely mean war. It was not long in coming. In the summer of 1640, the king sent a new military expedition to subdue Scotland. The Covenanters quickly reconstituted their army and readied to repulse the king's army.

In August 1640 Rutherford, a staunch defender of Covenanter resistance to the king, left St Andrews to preach a series of sermons from Isaiah 41 to the Scottish troops and to their supporters. 'Beloved in Him,' he preached as the Covenanter army prepared to face a large English force, 'in this chapter the Lord is looking upon a people that were weak, few, poor, and were also in the midst of their enemies. And the Lord knows well what are the thoughts of His children when they are in such a case.'

As he did in all his sermons, Rutherford pointed his hearers to Jesus Christ. 'The sufferings of the Kirk and the children of God,' he preached, 'they are Christ's suffering. But your sorrowful heart, your losses, your sufferings, they are Christ's.'

He implored them 'to fear not' because the Lord promised to help them through all difficulties. Ultimately, the victory depended on him. 'We believe certainly that the Lord will take vengeance upon the enemies of our Covenant in Scotland, and of this cause that we are now called to go into the fields for,' he said. 'The Kirk is victorious over her enemies because her head, Christ, has strength enough for Him and her both.'

The Covenanter army crossed the River Tweed — the border between England and Scotland — and like the year before, forced Charles's army to retreat. In the hope of pressing the king to come to terms, the Scots took the initiative and followed up with an invasion, seizing control of Newcastle and large swaths of territory in northern England.

With no hope of victory, Charles had to sign a humiliating treaty with the Scots. In it, he promised to redress the concerns of the Scottish Kirk and pay the Covenanters' war expenses. He also agreed that the Scottish army could occupy Newcastle and Northumberland until they were paid. Out of money and out of options, the king was forced to call the English Parliament into session. Having governed without Parliament for most of his reign, he now needed it to obtain the resources that he so desperately required to deal with the Scots.

The king was loathe to recall Parliament because most of
its members were Puritans who shared with the Scots the
same grievances against him. When Parliament assembled,
instead of providing the king money, they demanded
reforms in the English church and state. Parliament viewed
the Covenanters as allies in the struggle with Charles I. This
began a clash between Parliament and the king that led to
civil war and Charles's downfall.

Meanwhile, Samuel Rutherford and Robert Blair faced
opposition from the townsfolk in St Andrews. One man said
that the people of St Andrews 'storm and refuse to regard
any of Mr Robert's or Mr Samuel's desires'.

The situation grew so contentious that Rutherford and Blair
petitioned the General Assembly in 1642 to move them to
another ministry. However, the General Assembly knew
the men were doing important work and insisted that they
remain at their posts.

In March 1640, after living alone for ten years, Rutherford
had married Jean McMath. The marriage was a source of
great joy and blessing to them both. McWard, Rutherford's
assistant, said of them, 'That happy couple was eminent
beyond others in all holy conversation and godliness. Never
knew I any among men exceed him, nor any among women
exceed her.'

Within the first few years of marriage, Jean gave birth to
three children, but two of the children died before they
reached the age of three.

During this time, the English Parliament boldly asserted its authority with King Charles. By 1642, civil war raged as the forces of the king fought the army raised by Parliament. In common cause against the king, an alliance was forged between the English Puritans and the Scottish Covenanters. Parliament abolished episcopacy as it had been practised since the days of Queen Elizabeth and organized a committee to reform the Church of England. This gave rise to a remarkable gathering of the brightest theologians and ministers in Britain, and among them was Samuel Rutherford.

6

Westminster

'Contend for the faith that was once for all
delivered to the saints'
(Jude 1:3).

In 1643, in the midst of the civil war between Charles and Parliament, the English Parliament, comprised of a majority of Puritans who opposed the demands of King Charles and Archbishop Laud regarding worship as strongly as the Scottish Covenanters did, passed a resolution to reform the Church of England. It called for a gathering of divines (ministers) to recommend changes in the church's worship, beliefs and government that would be 'most agreeable to God's holy Word and most apt to procure and preserve the peace of the church at home and nearer agreement with the Church of Scotland and other reformed churches abroad'.

On 1 July 1643, about 120 ministers and thirty lay leaders assembled in Westminster Abbey in London for its opening session. These men would meet for the next six years and be known as the Westminster Assembly. Since one of their stated goals was to align the Church of England more closely with the beliefs and practices of the Church of Scotland, the Westminster Assembly invited the Scottish General Assembly to provide representatives. The Scots sent a distinguished delegation of men, including Alexander Henderson, Samuel Rutherford, George Gillespie and Robert Baillie.

'I am now called for to England,' the forty-three-year-old Rutherford wrote to a minister, asking for his prayers. 'The Lord knows my faith was never prouder than to be a common rough country barrowman in Anwoth. And that I could not look at the honour of being a mason to lay the foundation for many generations and to build the waste places of Zion in another kingdom ... Grace, grace upon the building.'

Most of the delegates to the Westminster Assembly were relatively young — half of them under the age of forty-five and just a few over sixty-five years old. The finest theologians in the kingdoms were represented. 'So far as I'm able to judge,' the Puritan pastor, Richard Baxter, said, 'the Christian world, since the days of the apostles, had never a synod of more excellent divines.'

Although the Scots were not voting members at the Westminster Assembly, they actively took part in the daily debates and served on committees which wrote drafts for sections of the *Confession of Faith* and catechisms. Shortly after the Westminster Assembly began to deliberate, the English and the Scots united their efforts to resist the tyranny of Charles I by signing the Solemn League and Covenant. The Solemn League and Covenant, drafted by the Church of Scotland's General Assembly and approved by the Scottish Parliament, established the conditions of the alliance between England and Scotland in their struggle against the king.

It sought to preserve the Reformed faith in the Church of Scotland and promote 'the reformation of Christianity in England and Ireland according to the Word of God in the example of the best Reformed churches'. The Covenant also advocated the 'preservation of the rights of Parliament and the liberties of the kingdoms'.

These were troubling times for European Protestants, for the Pope and the kings of France and Spain had not abandoned their efforts to crush Protestantism. Another goal of the Solemn League and Covenant was to present a united front of the Protestants of Scotland, England and Ireland. The killing of thousands of Protestants in Ireland during a Roman Catholic insurrection added to their sense of urgency.

When the weather grew cold, the divines moved from the airy Henry VII Chapel to the Jerusalem Chamber, a much smaller space with a low ceiling, a large fireplace and rows of benches lining the room. Built in the 1300s just off the western end of the sanctuary nave, the chamber had been the scene of Henry IV's death, and it was here that the translators of the King James Authorized Version of the Bible did much of their work. During the deliberations, the Scots sat together on the same bench.

The Scottish commissioners got along well and agreed in nearly all of the doctrines under discussion. Their fellowship with one another enabled them to carry on. 'Thanks be to God', Baillie wrote in a letter. 'Never colleagues had a greater harmony. For to this hour, not the least difference, the smallest eyelash between any of us in anything, either public or private, makes our fellowship much the sweeter.'

The debates of the commissioners took a long time as every point needed to be carefully supported by Scripture. Rutherford, a skilled debater, drove home his arguments with keen logic and clear reasoning. The biggest bone of contention came when the divines discussed church government. Nearly all the delegates wanted to eliminate the hierarchical government of episcopacy, but they debated whether Independency or Presbyterianism was the most biblical form of government. A majority of the delegates favoured Presbyterianism, but an influential minority supported Independency — a belief that the local church was autonomous and entitled to choose its own minister, determine its worship practices and exercise church discipline without oversight from a regional or national body.

Rutherford and his Scottish partners championed Presbyterianism. The Stuart kings abhorred Presbyterianism because of its association with the Republicanism of Geneva. They thought it was contrary to monarchy. The Scots, being the only representatives with experience in Presbyterian government, exerted great influence in the debates. They insisted that unity in church government on a Presbyterian system was needed throughout Britain. One of the strongest voices for Presbyterianism in the Westminster Assembly was Samuel Rutherford's. In one of his most important speeches, Rutherford cited the examples of the churches in Ephesus and Jerusalem from the Acts of the Apostles as representing a Presbyterian model. The divines soon realized that Rutherford's mind was a force to be reckoned with at the assembly.

In London, Rutherford viewed with dismay all the different sects springing up in the city now that the king and his bishops no longer controlled the churches. 'There is nothing here but divisions in the church and assembly,' he wrote, 'for besides Brownists and Independents — there are many other sects here.'

A majority of the House of Commons backed Presbyterianism, but most of the soldiers in Parliament's army led by Oliver Cromwell were Independents. To Rutherford and the other Scottish delegates, Independency posed the greatest risk to Christ's Church. They feared that if each congregation was independent and unaccountable to a larger body, then anarchy would reign. The troubles associated with the Anabaptists in the early days of the Reformation increased their concerns. Believing that a hierarchy of church courts which included ministers and elders was biblical and the most likely to preserve peace and purity, Rutherford employed all of his mental and oratorical powers to defend Presbyterianism and defeat Independency. The Scots reported to their General Assembly that there was 'nothing more pernicious, both to church and state, than the leaving of all men to autonomy in religion.'

'We are here debating, with much contention of disputes, for the just measures of the Lord's Temple,' Rutherford wrote in a letter to Scotland in May 1644. 'Thomas Goodwin, Jeremiah

Burroughs, and some four or five others who are of the Independent way, stand in our way and are mighty opposites to presbyterial government. We have carried through some propositions for the Scripture right of Presbytery, especially in the church of Jerusalem.'

'Mr Henderson, Mr Rutherford, and Mr Gillespie,' Robert Baillie wrote of his fellow Scots, 'all spoke exceedingly well with arguments unanswerable.'

Although Rutherford argued against the Independents, he referred to them as 'gracious men' and 'the best of the people.' He wrote to a friend in Scotland: 'Of all that differ from us, the Independents come nearest to walking with God.'

Some of the English divines held to Erastianism, a belief that the state should have a significant voice in church matters and that the power of excommunication should be held by civil authorities. Rutherford thought it unbiblical to give the state a role in church discipline and left the church dangerously vulnerable to capricious secular rulers. At one critical moment, during floor debates on church discipline, Selden, a leader of the Erastians, gave a lengthy argument from Matthew 18, trying to prove that discipline should be administered by civil authorities. When no one from the Presbyterian side responded, Rutherford said to Gillespie, 'Rise up, George, and defend the right of the Lord Jesus Christ to govern by His own laws the Church which He has purchased with His blood.'

Gillespie stood and refuted Selden's points, masterfully demonstrating from Matthew 18 and other passages that God had entrusted to church officers the exercise of discipline. Afterwards, Selden was reported to have said, 'That young man, by this single speech, has swept away the learning and the labour of ten years of my life.'

Serving on the Westminster Assembly involved taxing and, at times, contentious labour, and Samuel Rutherford confessed that he and the other Scottish divines suffered discouragement. 'The truth is,' he wrote, 'we have at times grieved spirits with the work. I often despair of the reformation of this land.'

In the midst of their deliberations, Charles I issued a proclamation, declaring the Westminster Assembly illegal and its delegates in rebellion against the Crown. The divines ignored the threat and pressed on.

Although the divines disagreed on matters of government for church and state, there was unity on the foundational doctrines of the faith. The *Confession of Faith* that they painstakingly produced over several years was a systematic explanation of orthodox Reformed theology, emphasizing the sovereignty of God in all things and divine election in salvation. Rutherford, who revelled in the fact that salvation was from first to last a gift of God's free grace alone, wholeheartedly supported the confession's explanation of God's means of drawing sinners to himself. The following paragraph from chapter 10 is one example:

> All those whom God hath predestinated unto life, and those only, he is pleased in his appointed and accepted time, effectually to call, by his Word and Spirit, out of that state

> *of sin and death, in which they are by nature, to grace and*
> *salvation, by Jesus Christ; enlightening their minds spiritually*
> *and savingly to understand the things of God, taking away*
> *their heart of stone, and giving unto them a heart of flesh;*
> *renewing their wills, and, by his almighty power, determining*
> *them to that which is good, and effectually drawing them*
> *to Jesus Christ: yet so they come most freely, being made*
> *willing by his grace.*

As the *Confession of Faith* took shape, the assembly decided that a catechism would be helpful to explain the central features of the confession. Rutherford, who had written a catechism for children when he was a minister at Anwoth, became an active member serving on the committees that wrote the *Shorter* and *Larger Catechisms*.

During his time in London, Rutherford preached to the English House of Commons in January 1644, and before the House of Lords in June 1645. His message to the Commons overflowed with the love of Christ. 'O, for eternity's leisure to look on Him, to feast upon the sight of His face!' he preached. 'O, for the long summer day of endless ages to stand beside Him and enjoy Him! O time, O sin, be removed out of the way! O day! O fairest of days, dawn!'

In his sermon to the House of Lords, Rutherford emphasized God's 'absolute royal prerogative'. Creation works as God designed, he said, but God can intervene at any time of his choosing. 'To the creature, the sea must ebb and flow;' Rutherford preached, 'the sun must give light; the fire must consume; the lion must devour his prey. But in all these, God may command that the sea neither to ebb nor flow, but to stand out as two stiff walls of glass. He covers the sun with a web of darkness at the crucifying of the Lord of glory. He orders the fire not to burn the three children, and the lion not to eat Daniel. And all these things must be because God has said they shall be.'

In the message, he referred to the civil war raging in the nation and did not hold back from blaming the failings of political and religious leadership in the crisis. 'Others say a rebellion against the king is the cause,' Rutherford said, 'but rather the not timeous rising to help the Lord and his oppressed people is the cause. The defection of both kingdoms to altar worship, imagery, idolatry, popish and Arminian doctrine, the Articles of Perth Assembly followed and practised in our own kingdom without repentance, the ignorance of God, people perishing for want of knowledge, both under prelacy and now, the not building of the house of God in this land, the backsliding of many after the covenant of God is sworn are the true causes.'

Parliament received his sermons with thanksgiving and commissioned their printing and distribution.

The Scottish divines suffered a great blow when their leader, Alexander Henderson, died in August 1646. The mantle of his influence fell primarily to Rutherford. After three and a half years, Rutherford and his fellow Scottish delegates longed to return home to their ministries in Scotland. 'We are so weary with our exceedingly long absence from our particular charges,' Rutherford wrote to the General Assembly, 'that we humbly entreat from you permission to return as soon as you may think fit.'

Eventually, the Church of Scotland let most of the Scottish delegates return, but knowing that Rutherford's gifts were needed at Westminster, they instructed him to stay and see through the completion of the work. As Baillie observed: 'For the great parts God had given him, Mr Samuel's presence was very necessary.'

Remarkably, in the midst of all of his work at the Westminster Assembly, Rutherford made time to write a number of important books. In his theological writings, Samuel Rutherford exhausted every conceivable detail with multiple points and sub-points which often overwhelm the reader. In the *Due Right of Presbyteries*, he made the biblical case for Presbyterian church government.

His book, *Christ Dying and Drawing Sinners to Himself,* came from a series of sermons he preached in London from John 12 in which he showed that God exercises sovereignty over all things, including the salvation of individual sinners. In this, and a few others of his works, he combated Antinomianism — the belief that the moral law of the Scriptures is not relevant for believers. Rutherford emphatically taught that Christians, exercising their sanctified wills, must turn from sin and obey the commandments of God. As always, he emphasized the loveliness of Christ. 'Would sinners but draw near to Christ,' he preached, 'and come see this King Solomon in His chariot of love, and behold His beauty, He would draw souls to Him. Ah! Words are short to express His nature, person, office, loveliness and desirableness.'

The Tryal and Triumph of Faith arose out of twenty-seven sermons he delivered on Christ's conversation with the

Syrophoenician woman recorded in the Gospels. 'Believers often seek in themselves,' he wrote, 'what they should seek in Christ.'

In his book, *A Free Disputation against Pretended Liberty of Conscience,* he argued against the Independents' call for liberty of conscience, claiming it would lead to the disintegration of civil society. Rutherford urged Parliament to impose the true Christian faith in a unified national church, using coercion if necessary. This was the widely-held principle at the time in Britain and the Continent. Rutherford's book gave rise to the mocking sonnet of John Milton in which he compares Presbyterians to medieval Papists.

> Dare ye for this adjure the civil sword
> To force our consciences that Christ set free
> And ride us with a classic hierarchy
> Taught ye by mere A.S. and Rutherford?
>
> When they shall read this clearly in your charge —
> New Presbyter is but Old Priest writ large.

By far, the most important book Rutherford penned while in London was *Lex, Rex.* The title of the book declares that the law is king, and he wrote it while the Civil War raged between King Charles I and Parliament. It was, in part, a response to a book by John Maxwell, the deposed Bishop of Ross in Scotland. Maxwell, a royalist and a devout follower of Archbishop Laud, had helped to write the Scottish version of the *Book of Common Prayer*, the worship book that had ignited Scottish resistance to episcopacy. Maxwell defended the divine right of kings, arguing that it was the biblical and long-established practice of Christendom.

Rutherford flexed all his intellectual muscles in defence of constitutional government and limited monarchy. *Lex, Rex* assaulted the Stuart monarchs' belief that kings answered to God alone, not to their citizens or parliaments. James I had written: 'It is treason in subjects to dispute what a king may do.'

Rulers received their power from God, Rutherford asserted, and the means that God used to grant kings their authority was the consent of the people. 'The power of creating a man a king is from the people,' he wrote. 'If the king has not the consent of the people, he is a usurper.'

The people voluntarily give the king limited power to govern for their good. 'They measure out, by ounce weights, so much royal power, and no more and no less.'

Rutherford argued that subjects were bound by the law of God to be loyal and dutiful to their monarchs. But if the king used his power arbitrarily, perverted justice and trampled the rights of elected assemblies, then, as a last resort, the people may resist their ruler by force if necessary. 'Power is a birth right of the people borrowed from them,' he wrote. 'They may let it out for their good, and resume it when a man is drunk with it.'

Rutherford made it clear that the people were not to rise up against a tyrannical king lightly or quickly. Citizens, he stated, were to 'suffer much before they resume their power'.

Using many examples from the Old Testament, he supported his claim that armed struggle against rulers who subvert the true faith was justified. Among the examples he cited were David resisting King Saul and Elijah executing King Ahab's prophets of Baal.

In exposing the tyranny of King Charles, Rutherford did not mince words. He compared the king to Nero and claimed that Charles was 'drinking the blood of innocents, and wasting the Church of God'.

His book provided a ringing defence of Covenanter resistance to Charles. When the Scots refused to submit to the king's unbiblical demands regarding worship, Rutherford recounted, Charles sent his forces 'inspired with the spirit of antichrist to destroy the whole land, if they should not submit, soul and conscience, to that wicked service'.

Rutherford's writing grew heated when he listed the violent persecution unleashed by the king who abused his power 'to command an idolatrous and superstitious worship — send an army of cutthroats against them because they refused that worship ... imprison, deprive, confine, cut the ears, split the noses and burn the faces of those who speak and preach and write the truth of God ... the man who is king, in so far as he does those things that are against his office, may be resisted'.

Lex, Rex was a book of tremendous scholarship. In it, he cited scores of Scripture passages and quoted from Aristotle, Aquinas, early Church Fathers, Protestant Reformers and post-Reformation Catholic authors. Condensing thoughts and brevity were not among Rutherford's strengths as a writer. But despite its length and complexity, *Lex, Rex* was widely read in Britain. One delegate to the Scottish General Assembly said, 'Every member had in his hand that book lately published by Mr Samuel Rutherford.'

Not every one approved. After reading *Lex, Rex,* the influential Scottish nobleman, the Marquis of Montrose, called Rutherford a 'seditious preacher' and claimed that he 'put sovereignty in the people's hands for his own ambitious ends — by his wicked eloquence and hypocrisy'.

It was reported that *Lex, Rex* infuriated King Charles. When his son came to the throne, he sought Rutherford's execution for writing such a 'seditious and treasonable' book.

While he served at the Westminster Assembly, Rutherford was joined by his wife and their one surviving child. In the summer of 1645, another baby was born to them. They named the infant daughter Jean, after her mother. But soon tragedy struck again — they suffered the overwhelming blow of having both of their remaining children pass away. 'I had two children,' Rutherford wrote a friend who had also recently lost a child, 'and both are dead, since I came hither. The supreme and absolute Father of all things gives not an account of any of His matters. The good husbandman may pluck His roses, and gather His lilies at Midsummer … What is that to you or me … if we could prize Christ, nothing would be better to us.'

By 1647, the divines had completed the *Confession of Faith* and the *Shorter Catechism* and *Larger Catechism* were nearly finished. Rutherford was well pleased with the work. He believed that all three documents presented an accurate summary of the central truths of the Bible.

After four and a half years of service at Westminster, Rutherford secured permission to return home. The Westminster Assembly sent him back to the Church of Scotland with this commendation: 'And now this reverend and learned professor of divinity, Mr Samuel Rutherford ... we cannot but restore him with ample testimony of his learning, godliness, faithfulness, and diligence; and we humbly pray the Father of Spirits to increase the number of such burning and shining lights among you.'

In November 1647, Rutherford and his wife arrived back in St Andrews childless.

The General Assembly of the Church of Scotland adopted the *Westminster Confession of Faith* and the *Shorter* and *Larger Catechism*s as their subordinate standards to the Word of God in February 1649. The English Parliament adopted them as well.

7

Division

*'Wretched man that I am! Who will deliver me from this
body of death? Thanks be to God
through Jesus Christ our Lord!'*
(Romans 7:24-25).

When Rutherford returned from Westminster to Scotland, he resumed his duties at St Mary's College. Soon the Church of Scotland's General Assembly appointed him principal of St Mary's College and then rector of St Andrews University. Meanwhile, his fame as a theologian had spread abroad. In 1648, the University of Harderwyck in the Netherlands invited Rutherford to become a professor of Hebrew and theology. He declined. The next year, without seeking his permission, the University of Edinburgh elected hm to the Chair of Divinity. He must have felt honoured to be selected by the university from which he had had to resign twenty-four years earlier. However, he wrote to the authorities in Edinburgh and humbly turned down the position. 'Cast your thoughts on some fitter man,' he advised them, 'and it shall be my prayer to God to send an able and pious man.'

The Church of Scotland placed him on key committees of the General Assembly and he preached often before Parliament. With a dozen books and treatises in print and the reputation of his fine service in the Westminster Assembly, Rutherford was the most influential minister in the Kirk, shaping the policies of church and state.

Rutherford took pains to prevent the esteem that many held for him from going to his head. Robert McWard, a minister who had served as his assistant at the Westminster Assembly, said of him, 'It was manifest to all who were but a little acquainted with him that his modesty and humility were such, that in all his most eminent appearances for God, he studied to disappear, lest he should by standing up, be guilty of intercepting any part of that glory which belongs to God alone.'

'Seek to be like Christ in humility and lowliness of mind,' Rutherford told himself and others.

'You must in all things aim at God's honour;' he counselled a friend, 'you must eat, drink, sleep, buy, sell, sit, stand, speak, pray, read, and hear the Word, with a heart-purpose that God may be honoured.'

Believing that every congregation had the right to choose their own pastor, Rutherford spearheaded the fight to end patronage, an old custom whereby noblemen or bishops held the right to choose a minister for a particular parish. He led a group of ministers who convinced the Scottish Parliament to abolish patronage in 1649.

In an age of great preachers, Rutherford ranked among the most popular of all. Travellers went out of their way to come to St Andrews to hear him. In 1650, an English merchant returned home and told his friends: 'I went to St Andrews where I heard a majestic looking man [Robert Blair] and he showed me the majesty of God. After him, I heard a little fair man [Rutherford] and he showed me the loveliness of Christ.'

The flurry of productive activity that characterized his life at Anwoth and Westminster continued in St Andrews. McWard described his work in St Andrews: 'He seemed to pray constantly, to preach constantly, to catechize constantly, to be ever visiting the sick, in exhorting from house to house, to teach as much in the schools, and spend as much time with the young men, as if he had been sequestered from all the world beside: and withal to write as much as if he had been constantly shut up in his closet.'

Rutherford was at the height of his influence, and prospects for the Church of Scotland looked bright. But the political winds were changing. In London, Oliver Cromwell and members of the English Parliament who favoured Independent churches controlled the government. They expelled Presbyterian members from Parliament.

After Parliament's army had soundly defeated the forces loyal to Charles, the king fled to Scotland because he knew that he would receive no mercy from the English Parliament. Members of the Scottish Parliament agreed to a secret pact with the desperate king. This agreement became known as the 'Engagement'. In exchange for Scottish military support, Charles conditionally promised to protect the liberty of the Church of Scotland by accepting the Solemn League and Covenant and establish Presbyterianism in England. However, Charles also made it clear that he reserved the right not to fulfil all his promises should he regain power. Rutherford and many others knew that his support of the Covenant was a temporary political expediency and counselled against relying on the untrustworthy and unrepentant king.

When the Scottish Parliament came to terms with Charles, Scotland demanded that the English House of Commons negotiate with the king for a return to his throne in London. When they refused, the Scots sent an army into England that was quickly crushed by Cromwell's forces. The defeat of the Scottish army led to recriminations against the men who had intrigued with the king. Most Covenanters roundly condemned the Engagement and the 'Malignants' who had instigated it. In 1648, those who opposed the Engagement gained control of the Scottish government. They banned from military and government service anyone who had supported it. And they turned Charles over to the English under the condition that he would not be killed.

When the English Parliament executed King Charles in 1649 and declared England a Commonwealth, it shook Scotland to the core. The National Covenant proclaimed allegiance to a king and now there was no king. Although Rutherford had written against the tyranny of Charles I, he abhorred the notion that citizens would execute their own king. In *Lex*,

Rex, he wrote: 'Lawful resistance is one thing, and killing of kings is another — the one defensive and lawful, the other offensive and unlawful.'

The eldest son of Charles I, Prince Charles, fled to Holland. Most Scots looked to Prince Charles as the legitimate heir to the throne. The General Assembly of the Church of Scotland protested the execution and sent word to the exiled prince: 'We do from our hearts abominate and detest that horrid fact of the Sectaries [Independents] against the life of your royal father, our late sovereign.'

The Scottish Parliament informed the nineteen-year-old Charles that it would accept him as king only if he agreed to the National Covenant and the Solemn League and Covenant. In addition, Parliament required Charles to pledge to establish Presbyterianism throughout Britain. But Prince Charles was reluctant to do so. He hoped to win the throne without having to kowtow to the Scots. Prince Charles's supporters in England raised an army, but the forces of the English Parliament scattered it to the winds in the autumn of 1649.

After the defeat, Prince Charles had no option but to compromise with the Scots. His mother told him to promise the Scottish people anything to win their support. 'Then free yourself at the first opportunity,' she advised.

In 1650, over several days of negotiations in Holland, a Scottish delegation pressed their demands on Charles. Eventually, he agreed to the conditions. One delegate later summed up the negotiations: 'We made him "sign and swear a covenant which we knew from clear and demonstrable reasons that he hated in his heart".'

Rutherford did not trust the veracity of Prince Charles any more than he had his father. Until he demonstrated a sincere commitment to the Covenants, Rutherford counselled against granting him Scottish support. When the future Charles II came to St Andrews University on his visit to Scotland in the summer of 1650, Rutherford delivered a speech to Charles and the gathered dignitaries. His concern for the Crown Rights of the Redeemer compelled him to tell the young monarch that God established kings to serve the interests of the people and that it was his responsibility to keep and defend the Covenants. As always, the king that mattered most to Rutherford was King Jesus.

At this time, Oliver Cromwell, a devout Puritan, led the English army. Before long, he would dissolve Parliament and rule with a new Parliament as Lord Protector. Cromwell had hoped to find common ground with the Scottish Presbyterians; but Cromwell's support for Independent churches proved to be an impenetrable obstacle.

When Cromwell heard of the Scots' negotiations with Prince Charles, he marched his army north. Despite his objections to the prince, for Rutherford as for many other Covenanters, Cromwell was a usurper. Rutherford threw his support behind the Covenanter army sent to stop Cromwell's forces. At times, Rutherford unwisely linked the cause of the Covenanter army with the cause of Christ. In a letter to a Covenanter commander, he declared that English troops fighting the Scots 'make war with the Lamb'. He went on to write: 'A throne shall be set up for Christ in this island of Britain and there can be neither Papist, Prelate, Malignant, nor Sectary who dare draw a sword against Him that sits upon the throne.'

The outmanned Covenanter army lost every encounter with the English. Yet, at Scone in January 1651, the Scots crowned Charles who had renewed his sacred oaths to support the Covenants. The Covenanter leader, the Marquis of Argyll, placed the crown on his head, declaring him 'King Charles II of Scotland, England and Ireland'. The English Commonwealth would not allow Scotland to establish Charles II as king, so Cromwell again sent troops to Scotland to prevent it. The English quickly overwhelmed the ill-prepared Scots.

In a desperate gamble to rally the support of English Royalists, Charles led a Scottish force on an invasion of England; but Cromwell's army annihilated them at Worcester in September 1651. Charles fled Britain, and Cromwell established military rule over Scotland, garrisoning 8,000 English soldiers near the major cities of Scotland and installing a military governor. Soon, Cromwell decreed that no new minister should be installed in Scotland until he signed a declaration of allegiance to the Lord Protector's government. Cromwell also encouraged Independency in Scotland. Rutherford and other Covenanters sent him a letter of protest. Later, Rutherford wrote a treatise decrying English interference in the Church of Scotland. However, it was the church's own internal divisions that caused far greater harm to the church than any meddling from the Protectorate.

Although Rutherford and his allies acknowledged Charles II's claims to the throne, they thought any support of him sinful until Charles repented and embraced the Covenants from the heart. Seeing the Scottish defeats as evidence of God's judgement against them, Rutherford felt strongly that the army should be further purged of men who had failed to fully embrace the Covenants. However, a majority in the church believed that if Scotland had any hope of pushing out Cromwell, they needed to unite everyone in a common defence against England. They passed a resolution in the General Assembly which asked Parliament to reinstate those men who had been barred from military and government service because of their involvement in the Engagement. Rutherford and a number of other Scottish ministers protested this action. The 'Protesters' and the 'Resolutioners' heatedly argued their positions in the courts of the church, in writing and from the pulpit.

Rutherford and his fellow Protesters charged that the Resolutioners had departed from the Covenants and contended that God would not bless the Scottish military if it included Malignants. In the Lord's winnowing of the size of Gideon's army, Rutherford saw an example for Scotland to follow. 'All the creatures, all the swords, all the hosts in Britain ... are without influence from Him,' Rutherford wrote. 'And O what of God is in Gideon's sword, when it is the sword of the Lord!'

The Resolutioners, who significantly outnumbered the Protesters, won over the political leaders. Parliament reinstated nearly all those who had been banned after the

Engagement. 'I see the nobles and the state falling off from Christ,' Rutherford wrote in 1651. 'I am broken and wasted with the wrath that is on the land.'

Although the disagreement did not involve the doctrine or worship of the church, it created a bitter split in the Kirk that generated fervour on both sides. Employing the harsh rhetoric of the day, Resolutioners and Protesters alike put the worst construction on their opponents' beliefs and motives. Rutherford and his fellow Protesters called the Resolutioners 'covenant breakers' and claimed that they compromised the gospel of Christ by supporting the dissolute Charles II and the Malignants. The Resolutioners called the Protesters 'schismatics and separatists'.

In 1651, the Resolutioners barred Protesters from the General Assembly and deposed three of the most outspoken men; but they took no action against Rutherford. The Protesters declared 'null and void' any actions taken by the General Assembly. The two sides organized separate presbyteries and, in a few places, even installed competing pastors in the same church. In 1653, when the factions tried to hold rival general assemblies in Edinburgh, Cromwell's military governor intervened and forbade the Church of Scotland from holding a national assembly.

Whenever Rutherford viewed the liberty of Christ's Kirk imperiled, he threw himself into the fray. 'He never was afraid of the face of man,' McWard said of him, 'neither knew he what it was to be silent when he saw the interests of Christ in hazard.'

The intensity with which Rutherford held to the Protesters'
cause and the fierce party spirit among his Resolutioner
colleagues evoked passions that led to separation from old
friends. Robert Blair, Rutherford's friend and ministerial
partner in St Andrews, favoured compromise between the
Resolutioners and the Protesters as a way to restore unity.
He took the lead in trying to heal the dissensions in the
church. Thinking his efforts a breach of the Covenants,
Rutherford would have none of it. At a Lord's Supper service
in St Andrews, Rutherford refused to serve Blair the bread
and wine when he came to the communion table, despite
Blair's entreaties. Blair was forced to serve the table himself.
After passing out the elements, he said, 'O to be above,
where there will be no mistakes!'

'Mr Rutherford', wrote Robert Wodrow, the great historian
of the Covenanters, 'was naturally hot and fiery.'

Rutherford recognized the fault in himself: 'I am made of
extremes', he once confessed to a minister friend. 'I fear that
you have never known me well. If you saw my inner side, it is
possible that you would pity me, but you would hardly give
me either love or respect.'

Resolutioners complained that Rutherford slandered good
men who held positions that differed from his own. Robert
Blair said that he would rather have his 'right hand stricken
off at the Cross of Edinburgh' than write the sort of things
that Rutherford had penned about the Resolutioners.

The contentious divisions raged on for years. In 1656,
Rutherford complained about the Resolutioners'

mistreatment to a Puritan minister in London: 'These men seek more their own things, than the things of Jesus Christ ... They persecute the godly, and in pulpits and presbyteries declaim against us as implacable and separatists.'

The bitter controversy grieved Rutherford and his opponents alike. He knew that the ill will he felt for his brothers on the other side would not please his Saviour. 'It is hard when saints rejoice in the suffering of saints and go nigh to hate,' Rutherford wrote at the time. 'Contempt of the communion of saints hides us from one another and Christ from us all.'

Rutherford said that he doubted 'if we shall have fully one heart till we shall enjoy one heaven.'

One day, during the height of the church tensions, Rutherford was preaching in Edinburgh. After speaking for a time on the bitter differences within the Kirk, he said, 'Woe unto us for these sad divisions that make us lose the fair scent of the Rose of Sharon!' Then he changed course in his message and began commending the Lord Jesus Christ. For a quarter of an hour, he lifted high the glorious names and titles of Christ in the Scriptures. As he drew the congregation up to the Redeemer, a nobleman shouted out, 'Aye! Now you are right — hold you there!'

In the preface to one of his last books, Rutherford reflected sadly on the years of division and the controversialist writings that it spawned. 'When the head is filled with topics,' he wrote, 'and none of the flamings of Christ's love in the heart, how dry are all disputes? Far too often, fervour of dispute in the head weakens love in the heart. And what can our paper industry add to the spotless truth of our Lord Jesus?'

Although Rutherford was nearly a lone voice for the Protesters' cause in his congregation and in the Presbytery of St Andrews, he never tried to organize a separate church or a rival presbytery. And in spite of his uncompromising stand on the issue, the Church of Scotland did not seek to discipline him or remove him from his posts. However, many branded Rutherford an alarmist who found dangers to the Kirk lurking everywhere.

In the midst of the discouraging controversy, the prestigious University of Utrecht in Holland offered Rutherford the Chair of Divinity. It was tempting for him to flee the strife and enmity of the Church of Scotland where the majority no longer respected his counsel. For several months, Rutherford seriously considered the position before deciding to remain in St Andrews. Shortly afterward, he learned that Colonel Ker, who had led the Covenanter army in their doomed campaign against Cromwell, was contemplating emigrating from the kingdom. 'Let me entreat you to be far from the thoughts of leaving this land,' Rutherford wrote Ker. 'But though I have been tempted to the like, I had rather be in Scotland beside angry Jesus Christ than in Eden or any garden in the earth.'

Despite great discouragements, Rutherford never lost hope in Christ or his final victory. 'Go on in the courage of faith, following the Lamb,' he advised a friend. 'He will come in His own time; His salvation shall not tarry ... the sun shall rise upon Scotland; but if I shall see it, or how near it is to that day, I leave to Him.'

Meanwhile, the friction at St Andrews University continued. James Wood, a leading Resolutioner and professor with Rutherford at St Mary's College who led the charge in the presbytery against the Protesters, grew so weary of contending with Rutherford that he arranged a transfer to St Salvador College to escape it. When college administrators suggested that James Sharp should replace Wood at St Mary's College, Rutherford strenuously fought the appointment. Sharp was a strident Resolutioner in the presbytery whom Rutherford did not trust, but he was appointed over Rutherford's objections. A few years later, when Sharp turned against the Covenanters and mounted a fierce persecution against them, not a few Resolutioners had to admit that Rutherford had been right about him all along.

Despite constant health problems through the middle and late 1650s, Rutherford wrote three more books while teaching his courses and preaching. One was a treatise refuting Thomas Hooker, the Congregational pastor in New England who asserted that each congregation should be self-governing and independent. As he had in several of his earlier works, Rutherford defended Presbyterianism as the most biblical form of church government.

In the other two books, *The Covenant of Life Opened* and *The Influences of the Life of Grace,* Rutherford explored his favourite theme: the irresistible grace of God in the salvation of sinners. He examined the works of providence and found God's grace underpinning all of his actions. Even in the Covenant of Works which God made with Adam, Rutherford saw God's mercy and saving love. 'God never loved to make any covenant,' he wrote, 'even that of Works, without some acts and outgoings of grace.' Even in the threats of the Mosaic Law, he recognized God's 'evangelistic intention.' 'The Gospel may be proven out of the law,' he wrote.

Rutherford strove in these writings to bolster believers' confidence in their redemption in Christ because it firmly rested 'in the old and eternal designs of love in the heart of God towards His Son ... the bosom darling and beloved of the Father.'

Meanwhile, Cromwell's Protectorate was drawing to a close. The vast majority of Scots resented the seven years of his rule in Scotland, and Rutherford never accepted Cromwell as a legitimate ruler in Britain. When some Covenanters took positions in the Protectorate, Rutherford considered them traitors to the Covenants.

Cromwell died in 1658. His son Richard, who lacked the support of Parliament and the army, proved incapable of ruling in his father's place. When he resigned in 1659, the Protectorate ended. Rutherford believed that its swift fall was a judgement from God for their 'corrupt sectarian ways for which the Lord has broken them.'

Little did he realize that the regime that came to replace it would unleash a violent torrent of religious persecution the likes of which Scotland had never seen.

8

Emmanuel's land

"'No eye has seen, nor ear heard, nor the heart of man
imagined, what God has prepared for those who love him'"
(1 Corinthians 2:9).

Declining health and ongoing division in the Church of Scotland marked the last few years of Rutherford's life. With all his weak body could muster, he soldiered on in his teaching, writing and preaching while continuing to rise very early for prayer and Bible study. His wife proved to be a great source of consolation and strength during those difficult times. Robert McWard said that she was busy 'encouraging him under all that befell him to stand and withstand'.

After Rutherford returned from the Westminster Assembly, he and Jean had three more children. Of the nine children that Rutherford fathered with his first wife and with Jean, only one, a daughter named Agnes, survived him.

Alienated from most of the university faculty and the ministers of the church, Rutherford remained a solitary voice of protest in the Presbytery of St Andrews, but ceased to be a prominent actor in the workings of the Church of Scotland. 'I am alone,' he said, 'though I know in whom I have trusted.'

Following the death of Cromwell and the collapse of the Protectorate, various factions vied for power. The political instability led a growing number of Englishmen and Scots to support the restoration of the Stuart monarchy. They negotiated with Prince Charles, who was living in exile in the Netherlands, to take the throne once occupied by his father. With promises of ruling benevolently with the English Parliament and assurances to the Scots that he honoured the Covenants, Charles arrived in London to a jubilant welcome in the spring of 1660. Shortly thereafter in Westminster Abbey, he was crowned Charles II.

Notwithstanding all his vows and sacred oaths, Charles II ended up ruling as his father had. When the Earl of Argyll, the leading Covenanter who had crowned him at Scone in 1651, came to London to celebrate the king's restoration, Charles II ordered him to be thrown in the Tower of London and tried for high treason. In August 1660, James Guthrie, a Covenanter pastor in Stirling, together with a dozen other ministers drew up a petition to the king. They congratulated him on coming to the throne and expressed their loyalty, but they also reminded Charles of his pledge to defend the Covenants. The authorities arrested Guthrie and the other petitioners and imprisoned them in Edinburgh Castle.

James Guthrie was a close friend of Rutherford. Rutherford had often visited Guthrie in his manse in Stirling. When news of Guthrie's imprisonment reached Rutherford, he sent a letter at once to him and his fellow prisoners: 'Very dear, and much honoured prisoners for Christ,' Rutherford wrote, 'it is the cause of Christ which you now suffer for ... but fear not. You are not, you shall not be alone. The Father is with you. It was a necessary duty you were about. Fear Him who is sovereign. Christ is captain of the castle and the Lord of the keys. The cooling well-spring and refreshment from the promises are more than the frownings of the furnace.'

Rutherford saw a whirlwind of persecution bearing down on Scotland, and he wondered how he would weather the storm. 'Though I be the weakest of his witnesses,' he wrote, 'and unworthy to be among the meanest of them and am afraid that the cause be hurt — but it cannot be lost — by my unbelieving faintness, I would not desire a deliverance separated from the deliverance of the Lord's cause and people.'

Soon Charles II, with the aid of a royalist-dominated English Parliament, reestablished the dominance of the bishops of the Church of England and moved to stamp out Presbyterian and Independent English congregations. Through the restoration of the Stuart monarchy, the Scottish Parliament regained a measure of power which had been denied it during the Protectorate. A Scottish Parliament made up of royalists — most of them Malignants whom Rutherford had never trusted — quickly did Charles II's bidding. These men, tired of the influence of the Presbyterian Kirk, immediately launched a crackdown on the Covenanters, especially Rutherford, 'the ringleader of the fanatics.'

In September 1660, the restoration government in Scotland banned *Lex, Rex,* proclaiming it 'inveighs against monarchy, and lays ground for rebellion'. They demanded that all copies be surrendered to the authorities. Anyone possessing a copy after 15 October would be considered a rebel against the king. Hangmen burned Rutherford's book at the Mercat Cross of Edinburgh and at St Mary's College in St Andrews.

In January 1661, the Scottish Parliament passed an act annulling all actions of parliaments since 1638 supporting Presbyterianism and the Covenants. In one fell swoop, it abandoned the National Covenant and the Solemn League and Covenant, abolished Presbyterianism, established episcopacy in the Church of Scotland and recognized the king as the head of the church. Parliament declared that the subjects of the kingdom 'were henceforth forbidden to renew any covenant or oath without royal warrant'. A crier shredded a copy of the National Covenant at the Mercat Cross of Edinburgh.

All that had been accomplished since the Presbyterian restoration in 1637 was swept away. Constitutional barriers to ensure a limited monarchy and protect individual liberties were gone. Soon, Covenanter ministers and members of their flocks would be driven from their homes, impoverished, hunted down and executed for their faith.

'Christ is a free, independent sovereign, king and lawgiver,' Rutherford wrote in response to the calamity. 'He cannot endure that the powers of the world should encroach upon His royal prerogatives ... It is a sad time to our land at present. It is a day of darkness and rebuke and blasphemy.'

After the removal of the late king,' one Covenanter summed up the situation in Scotland, 'both church and state have agreed to proclaim and bring home and set up this man, Charles II, who is now both an idol and a tyrant, to rule over a Christian people in covenant with God, while by many evidences he was known to be a heart-enemy to God and godliness, and, in all his oaths and declarations, a mocking hypocrite.'

The restoration of the Stuart monarchy brought many Protesters and Resolutioners together again in common cause for Christ. One leader of the Resolutioners said, 'Our brethren the Protesters have had their eyes open, and we have been blind!'

Rutherford's old friend, the famous preacher David Dickson, had been a leader of the Resolutioners. The rift it caused between them was a source of deep sorrow for both men. When Dickson surveyed the rising persecution from the king's government, he said, 'The Protesters have been truer prophets than we.'

At this time, Robert McWard was a minister at the Tron Church in Glasgow. 'I do this day call you,' McWard told his congregation, 'who are the people of God, to witness that I humbly offer my dissent to all acts which are or shall be passed against the Covenants and the work of reformation in Scotland.'

The authorities charged McWard with preaching treason and sentenced him to perpetual banishment from the kingdom. He was the first of hundreds of Scottish Covenanters who were exiled from Britain or fled for their lives. Many, like McWard, found a haven in the Netherlands.

Meanwhile, Parliament restored church patronage in Scotland. When Presbyterian pastors were expelled from their pulpits, ministers who favoured episcopacy were installed in their place. Parliament removed Rutherford from his positions in the university and the church, confiscated his salary and placed him under house arrest. His ministry of teaching young men was over. He prayed that the Lord 'Himself may feed the youths'.

The plight of the Church of Scotland troubled him deeply. One of his close friends said that his concerns about the Kirk were 'lying so heavily on his heart as to send him into his grave'.

'I am decaying most sensibly,' he wrote to a minister friend. To another he said, 'I am now near to eternity'.

Despite his weakening condition, he continued to work for the proclamation of Christ's gospel in Scotland. 'Be steadfast, immovable, and abounding in the work of the Lord,' he wrote to fellow ministers, encouraging them to set aside days for fasting and prayer. 'Our royal kingly Master is upon His journey and will come and will not tarry. Blessed is the servant who shall be found watching when He comes. Fear not men, for the Lord is your light and salvation'.

Rutherford acknowledged that the Covenanter cause was 'declining' and 'fallen'. He admitted that the Covenanters had made many mistakes when they led the church and influenced the state. 'Our work in public', he wrote, 'was too much in sequestration of estates, fining and imprisoning, more than in a compassionate mournfulness of spirit towards those whom we saw to oppose the work. In our assemblies, we were more bent to set up a state opposite to a state; more upon forms, citations, leading of witnesses, suspensions from benefices, than spiritually to persuade and work upon the conscience with the meekness and gentleness of Christ.'

To Lady Kenmure he wrote: 'The Lord has removed Scotland's crown, for we owned not His crown.'

In spite of the dark circumstances, he knew Christ would protect his own. 'Faint not,' he counselled a minister who felt discouraged and alone, 'Christ is a numerous multitude Himself, yea, millions. Though all the nations were convened against Him round about, yet doubt not but He will, at last, arise for the cry of the poor and the needy.'

'The Bush has been burning these 5,000 years,' Rutherford once wrote about God's preservation of his Church, 'and we never yet saw the ashes of this fire.'

To James Guthrie languishing in prison in Edinburgh, Rutherford sent another letter, encouraging him to hold fast to God's truth and look to heaven. 'For certain it is that Christ will reign, the Father's King in Mount Zion, and his sworn covenant will not be buried,' he wrote. 'Think it not strange that men devise against you; whether it be to exile, the earth is the Lord's; or perpetual imprisonment, the Lord is your light and liberty; or a violent and public death, for the kingdom of heaven consists in a fair company of glorified martyrs and witnesses of whom Jesus Christ is the chief witness ... Happy are you if you give testimony to the world of your preferring Jesus Christ to all powers.'

Rutherford closed the letter by encouraging Guthrie to entrust everything into the hands of his faithful Saviour. 'Cast the burden of wife and children on the Lord Christ,' he advised. 'He cares for you and them. Your blood is precious in His sight.'

A few months after he received Rutherford's letter, a hangman executed James Guthrie at the Mercat Cross in Edinburgh. From the scaffold Guthrie cried out, 'I shall not die but live. The Covenants! The Covenants! They shall yet be Scotland's reviving.'

Guthrie was the first of thousands of Covenanters to be martyred for their faith under the reign of Charles II.

In March 1661, the Scottish Parliament charged Rutherford with treason and demanded that he stand trial in Edinburgh. For months, he had been suffering from what he called 'a daily menacing disease'. When messengers from Parliament arrived with the summons for him to appear before the court on the charge of high treason, they had to deliver it to him on his sick bed. 'Tell them,' Rutherford said, 'I have got a summons already before a superior Judge and judicatory, and it behooves me to answer my first summons, and ere your day arrive, I will be where few kings and great folks come.'

John Livingstone said that Rutherford 'much regretted that he was not able to go and suffer for the truth he had maintained'.

Robert McWard reported that Rutherford lamented that his infirmity prevented him 'from sealing all with his blood'.

'Now my tabernacle is weak,' Rutherford told a friend, 'and I would think it a more glorious way of going home to lay down my life for the cause, at the Cross of Edinburgh or St Andrews; but I submit to my Master's will.'

When members of Parliament learned that Rutherford lay dying, they voted to expel him from his rooms in the college that he might not die on the grounds of the university. Lord Burleigh bravely stood up and declared: 'You have voted that honest man out of his college, but you cannot vote him out of heaven.'

'He would never win there,' shouted one member. 'Hell is too good for him.'

'I wish,' Burleigh answered, 'I were as sure of heaven as he is. I should think myself happy to get a grip of his sleeve to haul me in.'

Knowing that he must pass through the physical pains of death, Rutherford worried if he would remain faithful. 'At the beginning of my sufferings,' Rutherford said, 'I had mine own fears, like other sinful men, lest I should faint and not be carried credibly through. And I laid this before the Lord, and as sure as He ever spoke to me in His word, as sure as His Spirit witnesses to my heart, He has accepted my sufferings. He said to me, "Fear not, the outgate shall not simply be a matter of prayer, but a matter of praise."'

And so it was. An abiding presence of the Spirit accompanied him every step of the way. He told his friends that he often sensed the Lord saying to him, 'My grace is sufficient for thee.'

Through his final illness, McWard reported that Rutherford was 'filled with as much joy of the Holy Ghost as he could hold.'

From his sick bed, Rutherford composed his final writing, a short document declaring his personal faith and recounting the state of the church in Britain. 'Though the Lord needs not a testimony from such a wretched man as I,' he wrote, 'if I and all the world should be silent, the very stones would cry — it is more than debt that I should confess Christ before men and angels.'

His declaration praised Christ for his redeeming love. 'It would satisfy me not a little,' he stated, 'that the throne of the Lord Jesus was exalted above the clouds, the heaven of heavens, and on both sides of the sun, and that all possible praise and glory were ascribed to Him.'

In his testimony, he rejoiced in the Scottish Reformation and professed his faith in the confessions of the Reformed churches and in the Covenants. He affirmed his duty to the king, but always to King Jesus first. 'We acknowledge all due obedience in the Lord to the King's Majesty, but we disown that ecclesiastical supremacy in and over the Church which some ascribe to him; that power of commanding external worship not appointed in the Word, and laying bonds upon the consciences of men where Christ has made them free.'

Rutherford drew attention to the promises that Charles II made in order to gain the crown, but then so quickly repudiated. 'Our souls rejoiced when his Majesty did swear the covenant of God,' Rutherford wrote, 'but now, alas! The royal prerogative of Christ is pulled from His head.'

He concluded his last testimony with a word of hope for Scotland: 'Yet we are to believe Christ will not so depart from the land, but that a remnant shall be saved; and He shall reign a victorious conquering King to the ends of the earth.'

As he endured his final painful weeks, Rutherford put into practice the advice about dying well that he had given others. 'Die with all thoughts of Christ,' he once wrote to a friend.

Until the end, he meditated upon his two favourite themes: the beauty of Christ and the joys of heaven. 'My honourable Master and lovely Lord, my great royal King,' he said, 'has not a match in heaven nor in the earth. I have my own guilt, but He has pardoned, loved, washed and given me joy unspeakable and full of glory.'

'I feed on manna,' he told a friend. 'I have angels' food. My eyes shall see my Redeemer. I know that He shall stand on earth at the latter day, and I shall be caught up in the clouds to meet Him in the air.'

He said to one visitor, 'O for the long day and the high sun and the fair garden and the King's Great City up above these visible heavens!'

After exhorting a friend to press on in obedience to Christ's commands, he said, 'It is no easy thing to be a Christian. For me, I have got the victory, and Christ is holding out both His arms to embrace me.'

'I shall shine,' Rutherford told another. 'I shall see Him as He is. I shall see Him reign and all His fair company with Him, and I shall have my share.'

He confessed to some ministers of the presbytery, 'I have been a sinful man, and have had mine own failings; but my Lord has pardoned and accepted my labours. I adhere to the cause and covenant and resolve never to depart from the protestations against the controverted assemblies. I am the man I was. I am still for keeping the government of the Kirk of Scotland entire. Tell my brethren of the presbytery that all the personal griefs and wrongs they have done to me, I do cordially and freely forgive them, as I desire my Lord to forgive me.'

Then he urged the pastors to make Christ the heart of their ministry. 'My Lord and Master is chief of 10,000 of thousands,' he said. 'None is comparable to Him in heaven or in earth. Dear brethren, do all for Him. Pray for Christ. Preach for Christ. Do all for Christ.'

When someone began to recount all that Rutherford had accomplished in his ministry, Rutherford cut him off and said, 'I disclaim all and I look upon it as defiled and imperfect as coming from me. But Christ is to me wisdom, righteousness, sanctification, and redemption.'

'Let my Lord's name be exalted,' he said. 'Let my name be grinded to pieces that He may be all in all. If He should slay me 10,000 times, I will trust in Him.'

Rutherford told another visitor that he did not put an ounce of hope in his own works. 'The port I would be in at is redemption and salvation through His blood,' he said.

As his eleven-year-old daughter Agnes stood next to his bed, he told her, 'I have left you upon the Lord. It may be that you will tell this to others that "the lines are fallen to me in pleasant places. I have a goodly heritage".'

During his final illness, Rutherford's breach with Robert Blair was healed. Blair stayed often at his bedside. 'Appear for God, and His cause and covenant,' Rutherford told him.

'I have been a sinful man,' he told Blair, 'but I stand at the best pass that ever a man did: Christ is mine, and I am His.'

'What do you think now of Christ?' Blair asked.

'I shall live and adore him,' Rutherford answered. 'Glory, glory to my Creator and my Redeemer for ever!'

'Shall I praise the Lord for all the mercies He has done and is to do for you?' Blair asked.

'O, for a well-tuned harp!' Rutherford replied.

On 29 March 1661, Samuel Rutherford died. His last words were, 'Glory, glory dwelleth in Emmanuel's land!'

9

Legacy

'...so that Christ may dwell in your hearts through faith
— that you, being rooted and grounded in love, may have
strength to comprehend with all the saints what is the
breadth and length and height and depth, and to know the
love of Christ that surpasses knowledge, that you may be
filled with all the fulness of God'
(Ephesians 3:17-19).

Samuel Rutherford escaped the hangman's noose only because a deadly illness robbed him of the honour of a martyr's death. Thousands of his fellow Covenanters would be granted that privilege in the coming decades as they resisted the tyranny of the Stuarts. Many of them found inspiration and comfort in the writings, sermons and example of Samuel Rutherford, the 'Saint of the Covenant'.

Using wisely the sixty fleeting years God gave him, the highly disciplined and gifted Rutherford crowded into his span the accomplishments of several lifetimes. As his friend McWard said, 'Mr Rutherford seemed to be many able godly men in one, or one who was furnished with the grace and abilities of many.'

He stood eminent in the kingdom as a parish pastor, preacher, college professor, theologian, author, Westminster divine, ecclesial statesman and patriot. In all his roles he strove to proclaim and protect the true gospel of Jesus Christ revealed in the Scriptures.

As a tireless pastor burdened with the care of the souls, he filled his mornings with heartfelt prayer and sermon preparation, then spent his afternoons visiting his people in their homes, bringing them consolation, encouragement and instruction in Christ.

Through his preaching, he strained to proclaim the glories of his Saviour and bring many with him to heaven. Robert Wodrow, the celebrated historian of the Covenanters, surmised that Rutherford was 'one of the most moving and affectionate preachers in his time, or perhaps in any age of the church.'

In championing Reformed Presbyterianism and the liberty of the Church of Scotland, he willingly risked all to defend the Crown Rights of the Redeemer. He fought for the right of the people to have a voice in church and civil government. 'Rutherford was the strong brain, the intellectual fibre of the Covenant,' a nineteenth-century Scottish minister wrote. 'He was an out-and-out Covenanter, a protester of Protesters, ready by pen or tongue to defend the blue banner even unto death.'

Another called him 'a right royal follower of King Jesus'.

As a theologian, he played a prominent role in the deliberations of the Westminster Assembly, shaping the *Westminster Confession of Faith* and its catechisms — the most influential statements of faith ever produced in English. In his many books, he furthered the discussion of the Christian faith in seventeenth-century Europe, Britain and America.

During his thirty-five years of ministry, he wrote a score of books that he carefully prepared for publication. With the exception of *Lex, Rex*, his great defence of limited government and constitutionalism, they were not long remembered. On the other hand, Rutherford's letters — which he did not intend to be read by the public — have never been forgotten. He is not remembered primarily for his work as a preacher or theologian or defender of the church, but for his letters that exalt the Lord Jesus Christ.

Just three years after Rutherford's body was laid to rest in the churchyard of St Andrews Cathedral, Robert McWard collected and published as many of his letters as he could find — nearly 400 written over a period of thirty-three years dating from the start of his pastorate at Anwoth until a few weeks before his death in 1661. McWard entitled the collection *Joshua Redivivus* — Joshua resurrected — because he pictured Rutherford spying out heaven and bringing back a report as Joshua had with the promised land.

For the last twenty-five years of Rutherford's life, many hand-written copies of his letters had circulated in Scotland to the great blessing of their readers. Time and again, Rutherford's friends implored him to permit the publication of the letters, but he steadfastly refused. McWard says that the reason 'he endeavoured to suppress and conceal them from the world' was that Rutherford did not want people to think more highly of him than they should. What he sought to prevent became his crowning achievement.

The letters, first published in Rotterdam in 1664 and sold in Britain without approval from the state or church, proved to be a boon to the beleaguered church in Scotland. King Charles II's government bore down on the Covenanters, expelling pastors from their churches, driving people from their homes and executing ministers and laymen for their faith. Many a Covenanter minister hiding in the hills, or poor cottagers whose church had been shuttered, found a balm of comfort and encouragement in Rutherford's letters.

Ever since, *The Letters of Samuel Rutherford* have endured because they abound with the love of Christ. Through his personal correspondence, Rutherford's spiritual imagination soared as he contemplated the beauty of Christ and anticipated fellowship with him for ever in heaven. His letters, laden with deep biblical truth and rich Christian experience, have struck the hearts and gripped the souls of generations of believers.

Countless Christian readers have found the letters a goldmine of solace and instruction, but above that, they have the power to strip away the extraneous distractions that clamour for our attention, time and affection and bring us back to the one thing that is needed: fellowship with Jesus

Christ. One minister described Rutherford's letters as the product 'of a holy heart on fire with the love of Jesus'.

Alexander Whyte called his letters 'seraphic' and referred to Rutherford as 'a second Joshua sent to Scotland to go before God's people ... A spy who would both by his experience and by his testimony cheer and encourage the suffering people of God'.

Alexander Duff, the great pioneer missionary to India, wrote of Rutherford: 'He seemed to breathe a spirit of such devotion as if he had been an angel incarnate, and filled with such joyous transport as if he had been caught up into the third heaven, and his heart yet throbbed with the unearthly sensation.'

Charles Spurgeon often turned to the letters for inspiration. 'None penetrated further', Spurgeon said, 'into the innermost heart of holy fellowship with Jesus.' Spurgeon called them 'the nearest thing to inspiration which can be found in all the writings of mere men'.

Richard Baxter, the Puritan pastor who engaged in a running controversy with Rutherford over God's sovereignty and human will, nonetheless said of the letters that, apart from the Bible, 'such a book the world never saw'.

In 1857, Anne Cousin wove phrases from his letters into a hymn called 'The sands of time are sinking'. The first stanza summarized Rutherford's lifelong goal to fulfil the admonition that Paul gave to the Colossians: 'Set your minds on things that are above.'

The sands of time are sinking,
The dawn of heaven breaks,
The summer morn I've sighed for,
The fair sweet morn awakes;
Dark, dark hath been the midnight,
But dayspring is at hand,
And glory, glory dwelleth in Emmanuel's land.

For further reading

Those who want to explore further Rutherford's life, times and works may find the following list helpful. His theological writings are dense and daunting for all but the most intrepid modern reader so they are not included. Many of his books and the older biographies of his life are available at no charge online.

Rutherford's sermon collections and letters

Christ Dying and Drawing Sinners to Himself, London, 1646.

Fourteen Communion Sermons, Glasgow, 1877.

Quaint Sermons of Samuel Rutherford, London, 1885.

The Letters of Samuel Rutherford, ed. Bonar, Edinburgh and London, 1891.

The Tryal and Triumph of Faith, London, 1645.

Rutherford biographies

Coffey, John. *Politics, Religion and the British Revolutions: The Mind of Samuel Rutherford*, Cambridge: Cambridge University Press, 1997.

Murray, Thomas. *The Life of Samuel Rutherford*, Edinburgh: Oliphant, 1858.

Rendell, Kingsley. *Samuel Rutherford: A New Biography of the Man and his Ministry*, Fearn: Christian Focus, 2003.

Thomson, Andrew. *Samuel Rutherford*, London: Hodder and Stoughton, 1884.

Whyte, Alexander. *Samuel Rutherford and Some of His Correspondents*, London: Oliphant, 1894.

British church history

Burleigh, John. *A Church History of Scotland*, Oxford: Oxford University Press, 1960.

Douglas, James. *Light in the North*, Exeter: Paternoster Press, 1964.

Moorman, John. *A History of the Church in England*, London: A. and C. Black, 1963.